PATOS ISLAND
LIGHTHOUSE

*Let your light
Shine !*
Edrie Vinson

*Edrie Vinson
and Terri Vinson*

Terri Vinson

THE
History
PRESS

Published by The History Press
Charleston, SC
www.historypress.com

Front cover, top: photograph by Louis Borchers, Turn Point lightkeeper; *bottom*: Debra Madan.
Back cover: courtesy of the Coast Guard Museum Northwest; *inset*: Orcas Island Historical Museum.

Unless otherwise noted, all images are courtesy of the Orcas Island Historical Museum.

First published 2020

Manufactured in the United States

ISBN 9781467145060

Library of Congress Control Number: 2020930480

We dedicate this book to all the brave men and women and their children from 1893 to 1974 who served on Patos Island and kept the light burning and the fog signal sounding in the foulest of weather and the darkest of nights. At times, they risked their own lives to save others, while the light guided ships safely through the perilous waters of Boundary Passage. To the Coast Guardsmen and women who checked on the Patos Lighthouse to make sure the automation was working as planned. To the Washington State Park rangers who established the campgrounds and kept campsites clean and campers safe. To the Bureau of Land Management (BLM), whose employees patrolled and visited the island for decades from Memorial Day to Labor Day, finally opening an office on Lopez Island to better protect and care for our public lands. Lastly, to the Keepers of the Patos Light (KOPL), an all-volunteer nonprofit organization in partnership with BLM and Washington State Parks, whose mission is to preserve the historical, environmental, educational and recreational values of Patos Island and its lighthouse on the northernmost island in Washington State's San Juan Islands.

We, Edrie Vinson, president, and Terri Vinson, secretary, of the Keepers of the Patos Light, dedicate this book to all keepers, then and now. And may its light continue to shine on us all.

CONTENTS

PREFACE

Following the automation of the light and fog signal in 1974 by Clifford D. Thresher and Terry L. Lonholt, the Coast Guard moved its families off Patos Island Island. The Washington State Parks, too, left the island, only periodically returning and tending the campgrounds. In 1976, the *Bayberry* under Officer-in-Charge Robert C. McSwain came to Patos and removed all of the furniture in the buildings. He deposited them in a dumpster on the dock at Lake Union, except for one chair in the log office that he thought could be saved. Since the Coast Guard didn't want it, he was told he could have it, and it has resided in his shop ever since. Two years later, John A. Widgeon, officer-in-charge of the Coast Guard Station in Bellingham, removed the flagpole from Patos Island and installed it at his station. The Bellingham station moved to the other side of the marina, and the flagpole was gone when John returned in 1987.

The history of Patos Island Lighthouse is rather bleak at this point of its existence. The Coast Guard continued to monitor the automated light, but the fog signal was abandoned. The sometimes-violent weather, lack of loving caretakers and the damage of vandals left the buildings in a sad state of repair. By 2005, all of the buildings except the lighthouse had been removed. The triplex was burned down by agreement for a training exercise with the Orcas Island Fire and Rescue Department, hence the fireweed where it once stood.

Enter Gregario Teague. The year was 2004, and the BLM Salem District as under the direction of Margaret Wuff, the Recreation Lead. Nick, as he became affectionately known, was sent to the Lopez Island, Washington office, where he had occasionally visited. But this time, he came as a permanent resident to attend to the public land properties in San Juan Archipelago. Working his magic among the locals, as Margaret had watched him do, he soon had a following to help him with minor repairs and vegetation removal. He moved the office, so he had a nice two-room place where he could have helpers join him to plan new adventures to improve recreation opportunities on public lands.

Just a few years later, Linda Hudson and Carla Chalker, friends since their childhood and aficionados of Helene Glidden's 1951 book *The Light on the Island*, joined one of Nick's work parties to Patos Island aboard a Washington State Parks aluminum front-loading, beach-landing boat. Under Nick's persuasive guidance, the two friends incorporated the Keepers of the Patos Light in 2007, and by the following year, the BLM had funding for the restoration of the lighthouse, a National Register of Historic Places property. On March 25, 2013, all 1,020 acres of BLM public lands in the archipelago were designated by President Barack Obama as the San Juan Islands National Monument. The next year, San Juan County became the first county in the United States designated as a voluntary "Leave No Trace" area. The first manager of the San Juan Islands National Monument, Marcia deChadenedes, arrived in 2016 and, by 2019, had developed the first resource management plan for the area.

The Keepers of the Patos Light opened the first professionally developed exhibit of the lighthouse's history in 2017, paid for by a grant from the Lighthouse Environmental Program (the license plate people), and the following year celebrated the 125th anniversary of the building of the lighthouse. The San Juan County Lodging Tax Advisory Committee funded an exhibit on the Coast Salish and paid a number of administrative costs to aid in publicity for the celebration. On the 125th anniversary of the lighthouse, San Juan Publishing's Michael McCloskey published a collector's edition of *The Light on the Island*, which included the missing chapter the original publisher thought too risqué, along with an analysis of the book by Michigan State University PhD candidate Michael Villeneuve. The Orcas Island Historical Museum and the Orcas Island Public Library received a grant from the Washington State Library to publish a Patos page on its Washington Rural Heritage website, which included 482 entries of historic photographs and records, as well as articles from the *Islands Sounder* celebrating the islands' history. In 2019, Congress designated the Washington State National Maritime Heritage Area, and the Keepers of the Patos Light received another grant from the Lighthouse Environmental Program to develop an exhibit on the boats that served Patos.

Today, the Keepers of the Patos Light operate a docent program between Memorial Day and mid-September that opens the lighthouse to visitors and enlightens them with exhibits of the island's history and its keepers, then and now. The docents are shuttled from Brandt's Landing, Eastsound, Orcas Island by Washington State Parks, which also designated one of its seven campsites for the docents to use. Between April and mid-September, Washington State Parks also takes a monthly maintenance crew of Keepers of the Patos Light to the island to clean campgrounds and beaches and to remove vegetation from the lighthouse, trails and campsites. State Parks, through funding from San Juan County, has provided three composting toilets for sanitation, but there is no water or electrical services. The wharf has long been gone, but State Parks maintains two buoys in the Active Cove between Patos and Little Patos Islands. There is a nice little beach at the head of the cove, perfect for a skiff from a larger boat or kayaks and canoes.

ACKNOWLEDGEMENTS

Laurie Krill, acquisitions editor, History Press, Arcadia Publishing, graciously guided us through the process of writing and bringing this book to publication. Laurie, without your skillful direction, we would have floundered!

Thanks to those who helped us gather and interpret the information that our readers will find within. Specifically, thanks to BLM recreation planner Gregario "Nick" Teague for starting the ball rolling that has brought us this far. And to Linda Hudson and childhood friend Carla Chalker, who cofounded the Keepers of the Patos Light as a 501(c)(3) nonprofit corporation. Thanks go to Marcia deChadenedes, manager of the San Juan Islands National Monument, of which Patos Island Lighthouse is but a small part, for developing the resource management plan, which will guide us into the future in caring for our favorite lighthouse.

A special thanks goes to those who shared their family history and photographic collections with us, allowing us to piece together the story of Patos Island and its lighthouse. Thank you, Sue Miller, for the box of "Mother's Patos Relics," which contained the rich history of our first two keepers, Harry D. Mahler and Albert A. Morgan, and their families. Thanks, Sara Huston Culver, for the loan of the postcard of the mail boat *San Juan II* arriving on Patos. This photographic postcard was taken by Louis Borchers, keeper of the light at Turn Point on Stuart Island. Thank you, John Christensen, for sharing your experiences as a Coast Guardsman on Patos in the 1960s, for answering many questions about the operation of the machinery and especially for loaning a copy of the 1913 postcard depicting Patos Lighthouse and George Lonholt, its keeper, on the gallery. Thank you, Rupert V. Hagan, a Coast Guardsman who served on Patos during World War II. Thanks to Eileen Lorenz, who gave us the photographs and the stories of her father, Donald E. Fox, who served on Patos following World War II. And thanks to our own "Patos Bill," the vice-president of Keepers of the Patos Light, who served there in 1952 and 1953 during the Korean War. Bill LaVergne headed up the campaign to restore the flagpole to the military camp where it once stood. Thanks go out to Terry Geer, young son of Larry and Carol, who spent two tours of duty on Patos during the 1950s. Thanks go next to Dawn Alexander, our former secretary, whose childhood on Patos is well documented by her parents, Dale and Darlene Nelson. Following the Nelsons were Harold and Helen Faust, the unlucky couple who spent the 1960 Columbus Day storm on Patos. And finally, we are grateful to Debra Madan, past president of the Orcas Island Historical Society, who gave us her watercolor painting of the camas blooming on Patos within a few years of the automation.

There are also organizations that have been not only helpful but also very supportive and encouraging. Thanks to the National Archives and Records Center in Washington, D.C., for allowing us to photograph the pages of the journals, and its Seattle branch, which kept the Navy Inventory photographs of the lighthouse and other buildings at Patos Island Light Station. Thanks to the Coast Guard Museum NW in Seattle for use of its photographic collection, and especially to the Orcas Island Historical Museum and the Orcas Island Public Library, which allowed us to perform this work in their offices and archives. Without their help, it would have been mission impossible!

1

THE FIRST PEOPLES

The Coast Salish and the Early Explorers

W hen the first people came to the shores of what we now call Patos Island is shrouded in the mist of time. The natives call this time immemorial. Evidence from Orcas Island to the south of Patos tells us that some people butchered *Bison antiquus* as early as fourteen thousand years ago, when the Laurentide Glacier covered much of North America.[1] Archaeologists believe that an ice-free corridor set the islands to the west apart from the mainland and the glacier absorbed much of the water, leaving more dry land surrounding what are now small islands. We know from remains found in the San Juan Islands and Vancouver Island, British Columbia, that herds of ancient bison roamed the tall grasslands available to them on these small clusters of ice-free ground. Navigating in canoes or small boats, people landed and hunted the Pleistocene mammals and fished the seas for variety in their diet. Just who these people were, where they came from or what they called themselves is unknown. Due to the lack of particular identity, from this point on, we will refer to them as the Coast Salish, the people who lived here in historic times and, for the most part, live here today.

Just how did these seafaring Coast Salish peoples get around in times of fog and limited visibility? How did they navigate through storms and rough seas? What did they do when they were faced with whirlpools, such as those just north of Patos in the Straits of Georgia? Did they know, for example, that large sand dunes with north-pointing caps lurked deep beneath the surface? Or was that something left to Canadian geoscientists to discover in the twenty-first century?[2] Whether or not they knew about these large dunes, they did know how to navigate them. What about the sandstone reefs that nearly surrounded all the islands? What was the peoples' knowledge? How did they pass it on without a written language? Or did they?

One can surmise from bits and pieces of evidence that the native mariners had a heightened sense of awareness of the water and of how it looked, sounded, felt and smelled. They associated smells with certain places. But did they also have a sixth sense that we cannot describe? Tim Bellew said that he went from the Old Fishing Village on Lummi Island to Patos Island with his father and grandfather when he was seven years old.[3] "We made it to Patos in a fog. We used to go five times in the winter to harvest bottom fish. It was a way of life and supplemented our income. Listen to the water at Patos and how much power it has. It is a female current." "Look at whirlpools. They represent long hair." While Bellew told us little of the skills it took to find Patos in the fog, he was most observant of his surroundings and the meanings to be found in the native way of life.

Other mentions of mariners being gone during storms tell of the people gathering and singing on the shore, so that the canoers would hear them and find their way home in the dark or smell the smoke from their fires on the wind. Echoes, too, helped fix their location. Sam Barlow, a steamboat captain, used the sound echoed from a cabin on Indian Island to tell how close he was to the Eastsound dock on Orcas. And even the fog was not thick enough to block the smells of a village of people with their crops, their cooking fires, their animals and, well, their wastes. But how could one find an uninhabited island out there alone in the vast sea?

Water travel was essential to their way of life, and it continues to be to this day. Long after the lighthouse was built on Alden Point, native peoples continued to travel to and fish near Patos, camping on the beach at the head of Active Cove. They called on the keepers and gave them fish, or sold fish to them, depending on their economic situation. Each helped the other.[4]

WHEN THE FIRST EUROPEAN explorers arrived, they carried with them the best aids to navigation to be found at the time. They had maps and charts, spyglasses and the knowledge of navigating by the stars. And they made maps, took soundings and measured or surveyed their progress, recording their way from place to place and holding up when the weather was too bad to see. Still, the finest technology was not enough to keep them safe from the unknowns. The number of books on shipwrecks is testimony to the hazards of seafaring.

It was Spanish explorer Francisco Eliza who named the island Patos in 1791. The name means "ducks" or "seabirds" in Spanish. While many of the place-names given by Eliza were changed by later explorers, this one stuck. An American explorer, Captain James Alden Jr. of the United States Coast Survey, with his steamer *Active*, began surveying the U.S. West Coast. He arrived in the San Juan Islands in 1853 and in 1854. And in 1858, he worked for the U.S. Boundary Commission, placing all of Canada's Gulf Islands on the U.S. side of the boundary on his map. While he was not sure where the boundary would ultimately go, he did lend his name to Alden Point, where the future lighthouse would be built, and the name of his ship, *Active*, to Active Cove.

Juan Pantoja y Arriaga, another Spanish explorer, recorded that the waters around the point of the island were very treacherous, with "such whirlpools that without exaggeration there seems to be a small vortex." The wreck of the *Zephyr* demonstrates the power of such currents, coupled with a winter storm that typically starts with a southeast wind and then shifts to the northeast. The San Francisco Mint was under construction in San Francisco.[5] It arranged to have the sandstone for the structure cut from Newcastle Island in the Canadian Gulf Islands to the northwest of Patos. The *Zephyr* was

The Pig War. John Penson oil painting, 1905.

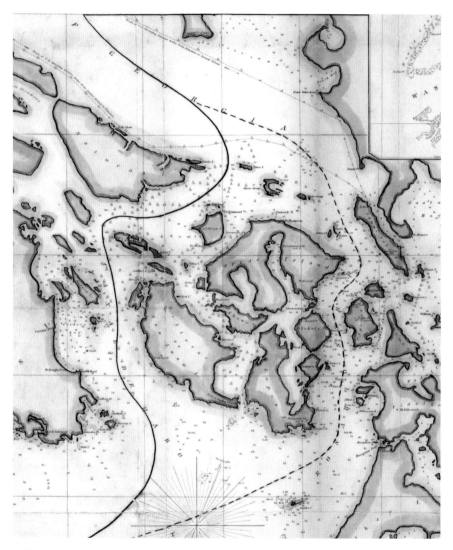

British and American governments vied for control of the San Juan Islands from the 1850s until 1878, when they were declared a part of the Oregon Territory. Patos Island is the tiny northernmost area in the disputed island chain. Drawn under the command of James Alden, 1854.

a three-mast barque built in Medford, Massachusetts, in 1855. It was the right ship for the job and so was brought around the South American Horn to take on this task. On February 12, 1872, it left Departure Bay with two of the eight sandstone columns ordered and several large sandstone blocks. The columns were ninety feet long and three feet in diameter and weighed nearly forty tons each. The large slabs were three by four feet each and weighed another 3,500 pounds each. The weather was stormy; it began to snow hard, the wind shifting to out of the northeast. The weight of the sandstone, plus the pressure of the wind, made the vessel difficult to control. It drifted westward onto a reef near Mayne Island to the northwest of Patos. During the night, the hull began to fill with water faster than the pumps could handle it. The crew planned to abandon the ship at first light, but the storm forced the ship to heel over and turn from starboard to port side, and everyone ran for the boat to get it out of the wreckage before it was smashed. Everyone aboard lived to tell the fate of the *Zephyr* except for the captain and one crewman.

The *Vancouver Island Pilot*, a publication by the Admiralty Hydrographic office in Vancouver, B.C., warned that Boundary Passage "was subject to heavy tide rippling and eddies." On the other side of the border, the *United States Coast Pilot* later concurred that "heavy dangerous tide rips occur between East Point and Patos Island and for two miles northward in the Georgia Strait." With this reputation for trouble, Patos Island was reserved by the federal government in 1875 for use as a navigational site to make the passage safe for shipping.[6]

While the demonstrated need was great, the governments moved slowly. In February 1886, the *John Rosenfeld* was being towed by the tug *Tacoma* on its way from Nanaimo, Vancouver Island, to San Francisco. Captain Cameron aboard the *Tacoma* lost his way in the fog and was off course when his ship, loaded with nearly four thousand tons of coal, struck bottom on a reef off of East Point on Saturna Island. It grounded at high tide, and as the water receded, the ship broke up. Stripping the ship and salvaging its cargo was the only option. The ship was new, valued at $75,000, and as time went by, the value increased to $125,000 and, finally, $150,000. The owners argued that the wreck was due to the carelessness and negligence of the tug officers. Port Townsend's *Puget Sound Weekly Argus* complained that the Portland papers would try to show that the wreck was "chargeable to dangers of navigation in our waters." One such paper says, "It will probably be found that the wreck was caused by dangerous currents, etc." The court agreed that the tug was at fault but awarded only $12,000 plus costs, which amounted to around $10,000. This amount was barely the cost of the two lighthouses that were later built near the wreck site.[7]

While the Saturna Island residents warmed themselves on the coal they stole from the hold of the wreck of the *John Rosenfeld*, two more shipwrecks of vessels carrying coal from Victoria Island to San Francisco occurred. In

John Rosenfeld on the reef at East Point, Saturna Island, British Columbia, 1886.

November 1886, the *Bernard Castle* struck a reef and limped into Bentick Island off the tip of Vancouver Island before going down. And in November 1891, the *San Pedro* went down near Trial Island, a little northeast of the previous ship. Both ships had hit a reef. Meanwhile, the English Parliament erected a lighthouse on East Point, its light shining first on New Years' Day, January 1, 1888.[8]

Finally, the U.S. Lighthouse Establishment made plans to take the sting out of the treacherous currents through Haro Strait, Boundary Pass and the Strait of Georgia. The *Seattle Post-Intelligencer* announced on May 6, 1890, that Portland-based engineer Major T.H. Handbury arranged for two new lighthouses to be built in the Puget Sound: a light and fog signal on Patos Island, and a light at Turn Point.[9] George W. Freeman surveyed Patos in 1891 and picked a spot for the lighthouse on Alden Point, just across from the East Point Light. Back in Portland, Carl Leick,

Alden Point, Patos Island, with the new fog signal station proof of construction by Foard & Stokes Company.

Keeper's residence proof of construction by Foard & Stokes Company of Astoria.

architect for the Thirteenth Lighthouse District, was designing lighthouses for the American side of the line dividing the two countries.[10] Two of those lighthouses were for Turn Point on Stuart Island and Alden Point on Patos Island. A brief description of what was to be built appeared in the Seattle paper on August 2, 1892, when Handbury requested bids for the construction.[11] Patos was to receive a "double Keeper's Dwelling, a Fog Signal Building, Cisterns and Draining. Grading, etc.," and the same, plus a barn, for Turn Point. Foard & Stokes Company of Astoria won the contract to build on Patos on December 27, 1892, and the following year, it submitted two photographs as proof of construction.

2

THE FIRST KEEPERS

Mahler, Morgan, Durgan and Lonholt

With a dateline of July 28, 1893, the *Seattle Post-Intelligencer* reported that Collector James C. Saunders announced the appointment of Ed Durgan of Whatcom as the keeper of the light on Patos Island and John O. Latta of Pierce County as keeper of the Turn Point Light on Stuart Island.[12] The paper went on to say: "The fact is not generally known that the collector of customs practically appoints the keepers of all new lighthouses established by the government. That is, his recommendation is virtually an appointment for these places."

Imagine the surprise on peoples' faces when, a few days later, Harry D. Mahler was appointed keeper of the Patos Fog Signal Station and A.F. Allen as keeper at Turn Point. Durgan, age thirty-five, had arrived about a week earlier than Mahler, age twenty-eight. To add insult to injury, Mahler was a single man. Durgan had moved his wife, Estelle; six-year-old daughter, Mary; four-year-old son, Clarence; and six-month-old daughter, Clara, into the new keeper's quarters. No doubt, both Durgan and Latta shortly thereafter applied for reassignment. But that had to wait; for now, Durgan worked for Mahler, and Latta worked for Allen. The difference was more than just pride. The keeper received $700 a month for his service, while the assistant was paid only $500.

Getting the fog signal up and running was quite a chore, requiring four months of intensive working with the equipment as well as clearing the land. On November 30, 1893, the first journal entry said that the stake light was lit for the first time.[13] In addition to reporting the on weather, the direction

Right: Harry D. Mahler, first keeper of Patos Island Fog Signal Station.

Below: *Patos Island Lighthouse. Watercolor by Kristy Gjesme, Green Winds Studio, Friday Harbor, Washington.*

the wind blew and all passing ships and their direction of travel, the journal was a record of other activities at the station. The very next day, the keepers cleaned the lantern and oiled the engine for the fog signal before returning to clearing land.[14] The next day, Mahler took a rowboat trip to Eastsound on Orcas Island for the mail, while Durgan surveyed the timber on the island. On the fourth day, the two keepers "went for a flag pole" of, no doubt, native timber. These first four days set a pattern for many days to come. A tug passed towing a ship, two steamers passed and a Whitehall with five Indians aboard went by. Mahler went again for the mail. And their first visitor, a Mr. Watlet, manager of the Tumbo mines, came by and stayed the night. The "2 Japs" with him slept in the boathouse. For them, what a cold and damp night it must have been. On December 19, the inspector arrived on the tender *Columbine* and inspected the station and left supplies.

One of the main supplies was a library. Since the keepers were on their own for much of the time, the U.S. Lighthouse Service saw to it that they had plenty of reading materials, including many how-to books. When there were children, schoolbooks for the appropriate ages were included in the library. Home schooling was common in locations where no schools were available, but the service was very considerate in moving lightkeepers to locations where their children could attend school. For the duration of the lighthouse as an active complex, the library was an important part of it. Relief keepers often commented on the value of the library on the island.

The winter of 1894 was one of rain, heavy snow, cold and sleet. In February, real trouble started. At about 2:00 a.m. on February 7, a gale blew over half of the walkway leading to the fog signal station, including all of the railing, and also blew out the stake light. On February 19, the water pipes froze. Then the pipes burst. The inspector had suggested a shelf be made for the lantern and a ladder made to make it easier to reach the lantern. Mahler was busy doing that. On March 8, the lantern blew out again. All the while, the place had to be washed, painted and ready at a moment's notice for inspection. At the same time, the keeper's journal needed to be kept up-to-date.

Durgan knew that his days on Patos were short, but he toiled at putting in the garden and keeping everything in tip-top shape and clean as a whistle just the same. He packed up his belongings and bided his time. On May 17, during a mail visit to Eastsound, Durgan returned with a Miss Baker and a Mr. Joseph Dunson. He showed Dunson around and even took him to Eastsound for a mail run. Finally, on May 23, he received orders to report at Point Wilson by July 1. As was the custom at the time, he went to Sucia

Island to try to arrange for a sloop to move him. Blanchard gave him a Mr. Lumberg to do the move. Meanwhile, on May 26, Mr. Dunson and family arrived on the steamer *Angeles* at 8:00 p.m. Joseph Dunson was the new assistant keeper, and his wife, Eleanor, and two sons, Ray and Claude, made up the family.

When military vessels passed, it was the custom to salute them by dipping the flag three times. The keepers did this when the lanyard on the pole wasn't stuck. Besides dealing with the livestock and their needs, tending to the garden and its yields and working on the stake light, they cleaned, painted, cleared, cut wood and worked on the foghorn. That darn horn never seemed to work or sound right, no matter what they did to it! But the most frustrating sound was the British man-of-war that liked to conduct target practice around 10:00 p.m. just north of the lighthouse. On October 6, 1894, they had their first white frost of the season. On November 6, Mahler went to Eastsound to vote and returned promptly so that Dunson could also go and vote.

Although Harry Mahler was a single man, he was not alone. Much of the time, either his mother, Anna; his brother Charles or "Charlie"; his sister (whose name we never learned); or his father, Gustav, were either there, en route or returning from Patos. They lived in Edison, now Skagit County, which is west of Bow and south of Blanchard, all three of which are south of Bellingham. They took care of Harry as they had always done—as a family. He spent much of this time shuttling them back and forth, depending on the weather and who could be there at the time. Charlie proved to be most useful, always helping with animals, on the land and on trips back and forth from the station. Their presence allowed Harry the leisure to join a lodge in Eastsound and to take trips there even on Sundays, when station business would not be conducted, to go to church.

Beginning on November 29, 1894, Mahler spent the evening in Eastsound by invitation, returning at 2:00 p.m. the following day. On December 4, he again went to Eastsound and, due to a storm, did not return until the sixth at 6:00 p.m. This pattern continued until he was invited to Christmas and returned the following day. The beginning of 1895 was no different, with frequent trips to Eastsound, nearly all of them overnight. Finally, on April 3, a Miss Rilling came back with him. There continued to be many overnight trips, ostensibly to get the mail. Then, he married the eldest daughter of dairy farmers Robert and Sophia Rilling, Louise, of Eastsound, on June 26, 1895.[15] That day, his log read, "Moderate to Light W. clear and warm. I went to Eastsound with Mother, Sister and Mrs. Dunson and was married.

From left to right, seated: Robert, Sophia; *standing*: Charles, Louise and Clara Rilling, 1980, E.A. Hegg, photographer.

Came back in launch with My wife and Mrs. Dunson, Mr. Dunson employed at usual daily work, mowing thistles along the walk." His mother and sister apparently made their way back to Edison. Were it not for other reliable sources, we would never know anyone's first name.

The Mahlers and Rillings were nearly inseparable. The local newspaper reported that Louise's sister Katie visited often, as did her other contemporary friends. And the Eastsounders made the journey to Patos, first with curiosity and then with great pleasure. Meanwhile, the inspectors came, too. When the inspector arrived on the lighthouse tender *Columbine*, the residences and the station had to be spotless, and the Dunsons and Mahlers dressed in their finest. Photos of the occasion made a record of the event.[16]

Born in Indiana, Louise was unaccustomed to living around water and did not adjust well to it. Yet she tried her best to be a good wife to Harry while remaining a part of her Rilling family in Eastsound. This required certain windproof changes to their launch. Then, in 1896, Howard D. was born into the family,[17] followed by Frances Louise in 1898 and Katherine Margaret in 1899. Her third child was born on Orcas Island at Eastsound,

Harry D. Mahler (*left*) and Joseph Dunson at the Patos Island Fog Signal Station. *Courtesy of the US Coast Guard Museum NW, Seattle.*

From left to right: Eleanor and Joseph Dunson, Louise Mahler, Katie Rilling and Harry D. Mahler at the keepers' residence duplex. *Courtesy of the US Coast Guard Museum NW.*

while the first children were born on Patos. Since there were two young children to be cared for, Harry rented the home of Isaac N. Waldrip on North Beach Road, not far from the Rillings, where Sophia could keep an eye on the first two children and also care for her daughter. When K. Margaret came, the local citizens lighted a huge bonfire on North Beach so that Harry would know that his child had been born. Although he reported each time his cow had a calf, he did not mention in his journal when either of the daughters were born. Every month, though, he reported when his pay came.[18]

Life on Patos was very busy for Louise Mahler. As first keeper's wife, she kept up her social visits to Eastsound and shopping trips to Bellingham and still had time for her chores and domestic arts. As a well-dressed lady, she made her clothes of silk and had many scraps from the endeavor. So, Louise made a crazy quilt of them and stitched them to a backing of the bags of many local flour and cereal mills. Also, note the lettering of the U.S. Lighthouse Service on one of the squares in the image on page 30.

From left to right: Frances Louise, Howard and K. Margaret Mahler, children of first keeper Harry Mahler and his wife, Louise, 1906.

On November 28, 1898, the *Columbine* came for the Dunson family to move them to Dungeness and brought Gustaf Anderson, an unmarried man, who took the assistant's job. Anderson stayed on until 1900. While the foghorn failed to work much of the time, the island was never very quiet. There were guests coming and going, the sounds of Mahler's cow mooing, newborn babies crying, the pitter-patter of tiny feet and the laughter of playing children. Add to that the sounds of Mahler's melodious guitar and the stirrings of a hoe in the garden. What a bucolic paradise!

Right: Louise Mahler, 1903. *James V. Bushnell, photographer*.

Below: Louise Mahler's silk crazy quilt. *Terri Vinson, photographer*.

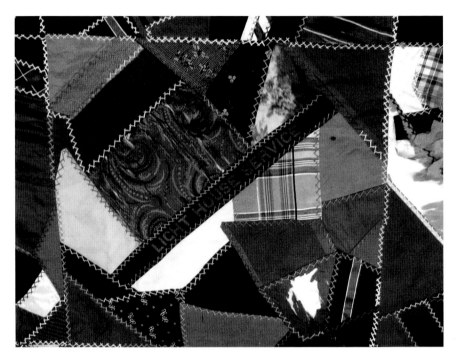

Above: Louise Mahler's silk crazy quilt. Note the Light House Service woven insert. *Terri Vinson, photographer.*

Left: Louise Mahler's quilt stitched to flour sack backing, Rye Flour, Lehmann Bros., Seattle, Washington. *Terri Vinson, photographer.*

Louise Mahler's quilt stitched to Seattle Cereal Company Fancy sack. *Terri Vinson, photographer.*

Albert Arthur Morgan became the assistant to Mahler in April 1900 and brought along his wife, Bertha Trahair, and children, Clarence, Francis and Lucile. Albert was the fourth person to serve as assistant to Mahler and the first to become keeper himself. When Mahler decided to move in order to get his son Howard into school, he left, and Morgan was promoted to keeper. Mahler had spent an entire decade at Patos, and the place had been home to his children, so it is not surprising that the Mahlers continued to visit Patos often while visiting the Rilling family in Eastsound.[19] The last visit was only the two sisters in 1969, and they were dismayed that their old home no longer was standing. Mahler himself stayed with the Lighthouse Service for forty years until this retirement, and his two daughters developed the nickname the "lighthouse girls." In 1984, the youngest daughter, Margaret White, painted a picture of Patos and glued it on a Christmas card she had made. The painting shows a light tower that was not there when she was a child, so it comes from memory of later visits or from photographs.

Harry D. Mahler reading the newspaper at his writing desk, guitar leaning on the side, 1893–1903.

1899 MY FIRST CHRISTMAS 1984

There is a small island called Patos that lies near the most northwest corner of the state of Washington, the meeting of Haro Strait and Georgia Strait. On it is a lighthouse that has flashed since 1893.

On November 25, 1899 there came a little girl to live and spend her First Christmas with a loving family—the father a lighthouse keeper, Harry Mahler, and Louise, his good wife, also a brother Howard, four years old and a sister, Frances, one and a half years old.

What courage this mother had to care for the needs of this young family, to make a Christmas on this lonely island, five miles across turbulent water from any shopping and food.

A SIMPLE AND PURE CHRISTMAS TO YOU ALL—THIS DECEMBER, 1984

Lovingly, Cousin Margaret[20]

Margaret Mahler White's painting of Patos Island Lighthouse, 1984.

Margaret and her older sister Frances LePoidevin, both then widowed, lived out the last years of their lives in a retirement home in Newport, Oregon, just across the hall from one another. Children who grew up on lighthouse property were by necessity very close, as their lifelong sisterhood friendship shows. Their dad began his career at New Dungeness before moving to Patos.[21] From there, Cape Meares came next, then West Point and, finally, Alki Point in Seattle, where they were both married and where Harry retired in 1932. He died only three years later. Louise moved in with her son, Howard, and his wife, Jeannette, to help raise their children.

On July 27, 1903, Albert Morgan became the second keeper of the Patos Light, now beginning its second decade. Boatbuilding was a popular skill or necessity out in the islands, and like many, he made plans to build his own yacht.[22] The building location was on the southwest shore of Patos Island, just immediately off of Active Cove. Boatbuilding and lighthouse work had to consider not only the dark hours when the lantern had to be lighted and fog season when the horn must be sounded but also the tides.

The building site was barely above high tide, but not above high-high water levels. Edward E. Pfaff, his assistant, along with his wife, Lulu, must have been very busy, indeed, to have allowed Morgan time to build his boat. Yet at the same time, he put in a very good day's work nearly every day he was there. And if he worked on his twenty-one-foot-long sailboat *Doris*, he recorded his time in the log. Everything was transparent.[23]

Several things changed under Morgan. He wrote in his journal, "my baby quite sick." "Still sick." And he took time off to take his baby, Osmore, along with his wife, into Eastsound to see a doctor. So, family matters were not left out of the journal. Also, holidays were not discounted. On December 25, Christmas Day, he wrote that "all had dinner with Mrs. Pfaff who had a tree for the children."[24] And on July 4, he took his family to the other end of the island for a picnic. When he returned, he reported in the journal that they had found a body of a "Chinaman," so he went to Eastsound to report it to the coroner.[25] The other main change that occurred was to the fog signal station itself. He worked for many days making concrete for the piers to build a new dock. And for the fog signal building, he built two benches, a table and a cabinet, then added molding to the interior. He painted shelving and the

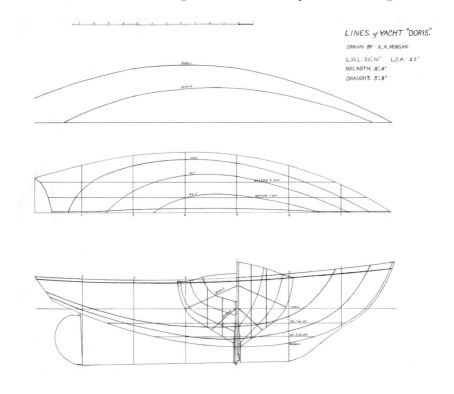

LINES of YACHT "DORIS."

DRAWN BY A.A.MORGAN.

L.W.L. 20:10"   L.O.A. 25'
BREADTH. 8:4"
DRAUGHT. 3:9"

Opposite: Albert A. Morgan's plans for the yacht *Doris*, circa 1903–05.

Above: Albert Morgan's yacht *Doris* under construction on Alden Point.

Albert Morgan's yacht *Doris* under full sail in Active Cove.

floor and put new shelves in the closet. Everything got a fresh coat of paint, inside and out, as did the residence. It was the first recorded major overhaul in the station in over a decade. All the while, he also reported the work that his assistant was doing. And each time he left, when he returned, he entered in the journal that Mr. Pfaff had everything in "excellent condition."

On June 27, Pfaff reported that Morgan had left on *Doris* under a light southeast wind in the morning and a party visited the station from Friday Harbor. That party, we learned from the *San Juan Islander* of June 24, 1905, was from the University Marine Station.[26] For the second year in a row, the university was using the Pacific American Fisheries Company cannery buildings along the waterfront for laboratory purposes. Dr. T.C. Frye of the university in Seattle was in charge, along with three other teachers. They had nine students—two men and seven women—who lived in tent camps up the hill from the cannery. They had two skiffs that they had purchased from R.C. Willis of Olga and two that they had ordered from James Scribner, along with the shrimp steamer *Zebitka* and one of Captain Newhall's fishing skiffs they chartered to move the group around. In a two-day overnight study field trip, they went to Patos, Matia and Sucia Islands for dredging and shore work. This is likely the first marine biology fieldwork done on the island. Later, the school built a more permanent facility on the north shore of the harbor, where it now resides.

After a trip to the Strait of Juan de Fuca, where Morgan apparently cut a deal, he learned from someone on the *Heather* that he was being transferred to the U.S. Customs Service. And, sure enough, Mr. Edward Durgan and family arrived on the launch *Salmonero* on December 6, 1905, and, on the next day, took charge. Morgan packed his belongings on the *Salmonero* and left the station for Port Townsend. They had essentially traded jobs.[27]

After leaving Patos, Morgan won races with his sailboat *Doris*. Then, in August 1906, three other men—E.C. Collins, Jack MacKinnon and B.S. Pettygrove—signed in the visitor's register as arriving from Port Townsend on the *Doris*. So, Morgan must have sold it. He also built a thirty-foot ketch.[28] Morgan was a bodybuilder, adhering to *The Indian Club Exercise*, as published in New York in 1866. Just when he exercised is not known, as his schedule was full. The hard work itself was plenty of exercise. Life in the customshouse at Port Townsend may not have been as demanding as work on Patos. Morgan's father was a lightkeeper. So was his sister Nettie. Both of them had grown up helping their father, Osmore H. Morgan, and she actually took over for her father when he became ill at Marrowstone Point Lighthouse and carried on as keeper after he died. In 1918, Morgan died of the flu at the border crossing in Sumas, Washington, just south of Abbotsford, British Columbia, Canada.[29] This flu pandemic was unusually deadly and was the first H1N1 variety of the virus recorded. It reached as far north as the Arctic and as far south as the Pacific Islands, leaving as many as 100 million people dead worldwide. It is estimated that one out of every five people who contracted it succumbed. Morgan's three oldest children had grown and moved on with their lives, but the "baby" who was sick in the journal, Osmore, was just thirteen, and John, only eleven, at Albert's death. Albert Arthur Morgan was forty-three.

EDWARD DURGAN WAS THE third keeper of the Patos Light and its best-known keeper. His fame is derived from several sources, the most enduring being the book that his daughter Helene Durgan Glidden wrote in 1951 about their life on Patos.[30] She wrote in the voice of the five-year-old child she was when they arrived for his second tour there, up to the eleven-year-old she was when they left in 1911. Her book, *The Light on the Island*, is true, almost true and pure fiction. The most repeated almost-true portion is that the Durgans had thirteen children. Three of the children named in the book actually belonged to their oldest daughter, Mary; one of them had died before they arrived on the island. The account that three children died of smallpox after digging in Indian graves was entirely untrue. They buried no one in their family on Patos. Instead, one child, Cecil Rene, died in a Bellingham hospital of appendicitis. Another untruth is the story Helene wrote of smugglers and the battle that ensued once they were caught on the island. That story actually had a real basis in fact, but it occurred before her birth and at Turn Point Light on Stuart Island, not Patos. And it was drunks, not smugglers, who caused the fray. Here is as close as we can come to what really happened. According to James A. Gibbs Jr., in the *Sentinels of the North Pacific*:

> One bleak and stormy night, keepers Edward Durgan and Peter Christiansen were "chewing the rag" inside the dwelling of the Turn Point Lighthouse. All was dark and bitterly cold, except for the little corner of Stuart Island where the lighthouse shed its beam. Somewhere out on the heaving tempest, the steam tug Enterprise was laboring heavily, towing a lumber-laden schooner toward Alaska. Ed Simms, owner and skipper, was in command of the Enterprise. It was February 16, 1897, and a fateful day it was for the likes of him. Before departing Port Townsend, he had experienced great difficulty in rounding up a crew. Many of the usual brand of dock wallopers had taken berths in the numerous ships headed for the Alaska gold fields. Simms took the residue from the local grog shops. After an hour at sea, practically every man aboard was well liquored up. As if the storm outside was not enough, the storm brewing on the tug was even worse. Quarrels and fist fights broke out. As the tug picked up Turn Point Light, the melee aboard had reached a climax. Suddenly the strain on the ships' wheel subsided. The rudder had snapped its cable and both tug and tow drifted dangerously toward the shore. Panic broke out among the crew as the big black rocks loomed up all around. Simms managed to cut the yawing schooner loose, and those aboard her dropped both anchors but the seas were so heavy that she drifted on down Haro Strait, dragging her anchors behind.
>
> The frantic blasting of the tug's whistle brought keepers Durgan and Christiansen outside the lighthouse to survey the situation. They picked up the running lights of the vessel and were immediately aware of her perilous position. Without hesitation they waded into the frigid waters with pikepoles in hand. The waves broke as high as their necks but repeatedly they rammed the pikepoles against the tug's hull to ward her away. Between the keepers and what little assistance could be had from the inebriated crew, they managed to get the Enterprise into a sheltered cove where she was

Left: Edward Durgan, keeper, 1905–11.

Right: Helene Durgan, age three, daughter of Edward and Estelle Durgan, circa 1903.

temporarily safe from the sharp rocks. Then the lighthouse men, water dripping from their storm gear, shoved a small boat into the surf and rowed out to the drifting schooner to get a line aboard her. A breeches buoy was rigged up and all hands reached shore safely.

Back on the Enterprise, *one of the drunken sailors suddenly went berserk, grabbed a butcher knife from the galley and held his shipmates terrorized. Captain Simms in desperation struggled with the madman and managed to divest him of the knife, but in turn was bitten through the hand. The rest of the crew then jumped the enraged sailor, and with great difficulty restrained him with a straight jacket. When the tired and worn keepers returned to the scene they made repeated trips in their small boat removing all the crew of the tug. For lack of room at the light station, the survivors were directed to farm homes on the island. The madman was chained in a hen house until government authorities were summoned to take him away.*

Meanwhile Estelle Durgan, the head keeper's wife, took care of the needs of the visiting sailors, and for three days doctored blood poisoning that set in Simms's hand as a result of the bite.

When repairs were made on the tug's rudder, she was reboarded by her crew, picked up her tow several miles down the strait off East Point Light, and continued the voyage.[31]

 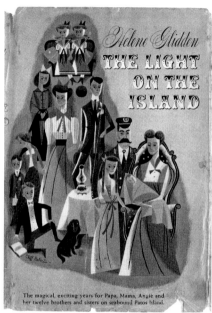

Left: Helene Durgan Glidden, author of *The Light on the Island*, 1951.

Right: Original cover of Helene Glidden's *The Light on the Island*.

Durgan got a commendation for this heroic act and, as such a recipient, became well known throughout the Lighthouse Service.[32] Another story Helene wrote, about President Theodore Roosevelt being there and staying in her room, is just false. The part about Papa being trampled by a bull was, unfortunately, very true. Another event, not covered in the book, made Durgan famous—or infamous—in the local area, depending on the politics of the reader. As told by *The San Juan Islander* of March 14, 1908:

> *FARCICAL TEST OF SUNDAY LAW—L.C. RUDOW IS QUICKLY ACQUITED*
> *Attempt Made to Convict Upon His Reported Statements to Friday Harbor Merchants*
>
> *S.M. Bugge and G.B. Driggs returned Wednesday evening from East Sound, where, much to their surprise, they were summoned by the prosecuting attorney as witnesses against their fellow-merchant, L.C. Rudow, charged by the attorney with having violated the law by selling goods on Sunday. The hearing took place Wednesday afternoon before Justice Stowers and*

a jury consisting of Capt. Gregg, Luther Sutherland, George Sutherland, Jacob Cramer, Robert Rilling and Arthur Langell. From the reports of those who attended the trial, independent of the "witnesses," who had not witnessed anything, the whole matter was about as farcical as the trial of A. Stoliker a year or so ago, when the attorney was "skinned" by the barber. Messrs. Bugge and Driggs and Sheriff Delaney were the only "witnesses" placed on the stand by the prosecution and none were called by Mr. Rudow. The complaint seems to have been founded upon the hearsay report that Mr. Rudow, when here last week, had said that he had sold goods on the previous Sunday to keepers of the Patos Island light station, and that he would do so again under the same circumstances. Neither Mr. Bugge nor Mr. Driggs would swear that Mr. Rudow had made any statement with reference to any particular Sunday, and neither could say upon his personal knowledge whether Mr. Rudow had ever sold any goods on any Sunday. Mr. Rudow himself denied having made the sale complained of on the Sunday in question, but frankly admitted having accommodated customers from a distance by opening his store and letting them have goods on Sunday and he said he would do so again if he pleased, simply as a matter of accommodation. He furthermore said that he had been bothered more by the prosecuting attorney himself, during his sojourn at East Sound last summer, asking him to open his store on Sundays and get him "five cents worth of goods" than he had ever been by anyone else. After this statement was made the attorney refrained from pressing this line of inquiry further. It did not appear that any effort had been made to obtain the testimony of the men to whom it was alleged that goods had been sold on the day designated in the complaint. Another hearsay witness, W.E. Armstrong, of West Sound, for whom a subpoena had been issued, was absent, having gone to Seattle.

It took the jury but a moment or two to return a verdict of "not guilty." Mr. Rudow was represented by Attorney H.C. Thompson.[33]

W.R. Garrett was the prosecuting attorney in San Juan County, and the keepers were Edward Durgan and Louis A. Pettersen (assistant).[34] The journal does not show any trips to Eastsound just before this date. The Sunday, March 8 entry reads: "Calm and clear. Sunday. Usual station duties. Keeper and son captured a flock of tame geese." It is also interesting that nearly everyone mentioned in the newspaper account at some point visited the Durgans as their guests. In fact, Edward was a very popular guy, with many friends calling at his station. Helene described her father in the book as "a fiery little Frenchman; his hands often conveyed more of his thoughts than his speech brought out." He wasn't French, and probably wasn't little, but he was a good keeper. And he was a good man.

One of the first things he did after taking charge of the station on December 7, 1905, was to invite Edward and Lulu Pfaff, the assistant, to Christmas dinner.[35] They also spent New Year's Eve together, and Edward Durgan (or his wife, if Helene is believable here) wrote in the journal, "Good by old year." Durgan and Pfaff and their families got along famously, making their life on the island a pure delight. Durgan reported what both of them were doing every day, and it is clear that he had great respect for not only the man but also his work. On March 13, 1906, the *Heather* inspected the station and brought Louis A. Pettersen as assistant, as well as his wife, Cheastie, and picked up Pfaff; his wife, Lulu; and their new daughter, Lucile, as well as their household goods, to move them to the brand-new Burrows Island Lighthouse. Pfaff would be its first assistant keeper, serving under Captain J.B. Hermann. Undoubtedly, Durgan's reporting of Pfaff's work helped him get the appointment, and Pfaff's own performance in 1907 led him to be appointed keeper in place.

The best to be said for Louis Pettersen is that the thing Durgan hated most, going to Eastsound for the mail, was what Pettersen called a wonderful day. He would likely have preferred to be a seafarer rather than a lightkeeper. He made or was gone for 210 trips or days before the steamer *Elmo* started delivering mail on October 12, 1908, and again 24 more days before he left the station on February 11, 1909. Durgan had been actively engaged in trying to get mail service on Patos, traveling even to Portland to meet with officials there to persuade them of the need. When the mail service finally began, he did write in the journal on each occasion that the *Elmo* failed to come or passed by without stopping. While Durgan did not openly complain about Pettersen being gone so much, he did on occasion write in the journal, "Pettersen busy with his own affairs." Besides the constant traveling, Pettersen's nephew from Norway came to visit, staying seven months. In addition to the nephew, a Mr. Aksel Andersen of Sucia, also a Norwegian, spent every weekend with Pettersen, so rarely did he ever put in a full day's work at the lighthouse. When he wasn't traveling, he was working on his boat. His wife traveled with him, unless there was a man to go along, in which case she was left behind.

On January 26, 1906, when the Durgans were still new on the island, a steamer nearly ran onto the point in a very thick fog. It could not see the light or hear the foghorn. Again, on October 15, 1907, a large steamer nearly ran ashore near the dwelling in a bad fog—again, unable to hear the fog signal or see the light. The foghorn continued to be a problem, and Durgan was constantly working with it. The *Columbine* brought cooling tanks for the foghorn in an attempt to see if that would help it work better. In spite of the time the signal took, Durgan and his family were very diligent in getting the station work done. In November 1906, U. Sebree, naval secretary of the U.S. Lighthouse Board, inspected and reported that everything was "very neat & clean in Excellent Condition." Later that same month, a friend, "Mr. Farvie came to station with badly scalded face. We assisted and made him comfortable." On another occasion, a steamer had run on the rocks on the south side of the island and Durgan worked to get them off. And if someone lost their load of lumber, Durgan would go out and round it up so they could come back and get it. He did the same thing for lost reef nets. He even went out and caught the buoys that were supposed to be marking reefs in Canada. Service to others, as well as to his family and station, was ever a part of Edward Durgan's life.

On November 2, 1907, the *Columbine* arrived with Carl Leick aboard to survey the site for a light tower. Leick was the architect from the Portland office who drew the plans for most of the lighthouses in Washington and Oregon, including Patos and Turn Point. In February, the lighthouse tender returned with the lumber and again in March with more building materials. The workmen began construction. A Mr. Warrack was in charge of construction, and a Mr. Wiltshire was in charge of the blasting that needed to be done to place a proper foundation for the wooden structure. A tinner was in charge of the copper for the tower roof. Durgan was busy with other station duties and left the carpenters to themselves until they requested his help. He did help them hoist the iron that would hold the lantern and with the painting of the tower. Once they were finished and packed up and had returned to their base, he spent the entire day cleaning up after them and many days finishing up the painting and cleaning the paint drips off the floor.

The *Columbine* arrived on September 15, bringing the lens itself. Major J. McIndoe and Warrack inspected the new lighthouse. The *Columbine* came again in October with E.E. Sherman to install the lens and to teach the keeper how to operate it. Durgan lit the new light on December 2, 1908, less than three years after the near crash on the point, but fifteen years and three days after the first stake light had been lit on the island. Sherman returned on the *Columbine* to check on the new vapor light and ensure it was working properly.

The new lens was a fourth-order Fresnel. The lens that lit the way around the world was invented by Augustin Fresnel (1788–1827), a young man from

Left: Fourth-order Fresnel lens in Patos Island lighthouse. *Photograph by Dale Nelson.*

Below: The base of the lens (the tower room is too small to include entire photograph). *Photograph by Dale Nelson.*

Normandy who was a genius at the physics of light. He was the first to believe that light was not a particle but a wave.[36] (Actually, it is both.) While he experimented with light and diffraction patterns for various-shaped edges, he recognized that he needed a system of lenses in steps, using "dioptric" (refraction) and the perfection of "catoptric" (reflection). Operating at a time before the Industrial Revolution in France, with literally a horse-powered turnstile, he struggled to manufacture the vision he applied to paper. Using inferior crown glass rather than flawless, heavier and more expensive flint, he needed blemish-free glass in sizes and shapes never before made, including the first flash panel with polygonal prisms and trapezoidal lenses. Because he was plagued with defective glass, imprecise manufacturing and poorly cast pieces, he resorted to doing some of the work himself. Ultimately, he produced the first lens in 1823 for the Cordouan Lighthouse. It was lauded for its brilliance, and he continued to strive for excellence, combining both the refraction and reflection lenses. His goal was to construct or re-light fifty-one lighthouses along the coast of France.

Fresnel died of tuberculosis, leaving unresolved questions about improvements he hoped to bring about. His younger brother Leonor took over the work for the next twenty years to bring those dreams to fruition. The lights he created were from the largest (first order), visible for more than forty miles, to the smallest (sixth order) for small harbors. Within one hundred years, more than ten thousand such lenses were in operation.

According to Clarence "Tee" Titterington, a Coasty on Patos from 1951 to 1953, "The light had a glass prism, a 300-watt bulb, floating on mercury to keep it level, produced 40,000 candle power and could be seen 7 miles away." He thought it was one of only two lights like it, the other being on the East Coast. Today, it has a modern lens, having been automated in 1974. It flashes a white light once every six seconds and has two red sectors marking dangerous shoals off the point of the island. It is battery operated, and solar panels recharge the battery.

Turning a fog signal station into a lighthouse was the hallmark of Durgan's career. And his reward was the happiest days of his life. When the *America* arrived in February 1909 to take Mr. Pettersen away, it brought Noah Alexander Clark and his family to the island to serve as assistant. Uncle Al, as Angie called him in the book *The Light on the Island*, was married to Durgan's oldest daughter, Mary, who, with his grandson Noel, was his extended family. Before leaving, Pettersen sold his launch the *Sea Pigeon* to William Coutts of Sucia Island. Coutts first showed up on Patos in 1907 and endeared himself to everyone he met.[37] He and Durgan were close, and he became very close to the Clarks as well. Durgan's oldest son, Clarence, who was third assistant keeper at Destruction Island, came home on the launch *Bermuda* with a new bride, Margery. And Roy came home on the *Canal Kitty*. The two sons had grown up with their father working at the lighthouse and were themselves quite capable young men. When they were around home for a visit, they always made themselves useful, lightening the load their father and mother carried. Feeling free to get around, Durgan went to Bellingham and came home with a new Imperial engine for the fog signal. That was the fix the fog signal needed. Meanwhile, the journal contained all the help and what the family contributed to the lighthouse operation.

All was not work, however. The journal also attests to their many visits to other lighthouses and other islands near and farther away. Al Clark and the Durgan boys were out in his launch when they encountered gunfire from the launch *Petrel*. They narrowly escaped injury, but the incident became fodder for Helene's book. The next day, they celebrated the Fourth of July with a picnic at the head of the bay. Later that month, on a Sunday, a large party from Waldron called on the Durgans and Clarks. August was even better. One day, the entire group of them took a ride around the island. The Coutts brothers came over for a visit, which was repaid by a visit to Sucia the following day. Then Blanchard and Clark went to the Carlisle fish cannery and returned with a winter's supply of salmon to smoke. Everyone was involved, cleaning fish and working the smoker, then storing the smoked fish. Once those were safely cared for, Clark brought another load, and the energy began again. And with that finished, the Clark family took most of the Durgans and visited East Point Lighthouse.

Indian Tom camped at the head of the bay, and Clark took the others to Eastsound and then to Matia to get fruit to put up for the winter. And Coutts paid a visit with his launch *Sea Pigeon*. Cecil Rene, Durgan's son, had a painful experience with his right side, and his father took him to Bellingham to the hospital. Sadly, his appendix burst, and he died shortly thereafter. The entire family went to Bellingham for the funeral.

As spring began to set in, the *Columbine* arrived with screen doors and windows, and a group of lighthouse men visited Durgan and the lighthouse. Durgan removed the old lamppost on the point, and a boatload of Indians camped on the island. The revenue cutter *Guard* came by for a visit and spent the night in the bay. Next, the tender *Heather* came to pay respects and inspect the station. While they were there, the Georgeson family from the East Point Lighthouse on Saturna came for a visit. Clark took the family over to North Beach to get some chickens from Mrs. Waldrip at the Mount Baker farm. And Billy Coutts took some of the folks to a dance, not returning until 5:00 a.m. the next morning. On July 1, the keeper and his family, and a party of friends, went to British Columbia to attend the annual Dominion Day dance, returning the next day at 1:00 p.m. Then on the Fourth of July, they "hoisted the flag in honor of the day and all enjoyed grand time from dinner with Misses Rash of Parksville, B.C. and a party of friends from Saturna Lighthouse, and Mr. Coutts from Sucia." The party continued into the afternoon, and all went to Lummi Park for a dance, getting home again at 4:30 a.m. the following day. Two weeks later, they went back for another dance, seeing lots of visitors and social activities.

On August 17, the schooner *Wanderer* went aground on the south side of Patos, and the keeper was there to help it off. The incident caused considerable damage, and the boat was held up for nearly a week with the extensive repairs. Coutts took the Clarks and the keeper's family to Saturna, then took them fishing for a day. Again, they made their runs to Eastsound and Matia for fruit to put up for the winter. In October, they were busy picking and storing their own apples, then took a trip to Mayne Island, B.C., to attend another dance. Thanksgiving was spent with the Georgesons at East Point, along with Clark's brother Daniel, who stayed around for his thirty-day vacation and helped out at the station. For Christmas, they "cut and fixed" a Christmas tree.

Then, sadly, the party ended and the *Manzanita* came to collect Edward Durgan and his family and move them to Blaine, where he ran the Semiahmoo Harbor light. The following day, February 23, 1911, the *Manzanita* returned with George L. Lonholt, a single man, as the new keeper. Lonholt went back to Semiahmoo for inspection and then back to Patos, where it, too, was inspected.[38] This is the first time that the keepers recorded the conditions of the lighthouse as a part of their reassignment. Lonholt wrote that the station was in very good condition. Even the foghorn was working fine. The assistant, Noah Clark, wasn't mentioned in the journal after the change in command until April 30, a Sunday, when Lonholt reported that Clark made a mooring buoy for the harbor, and on another Sunday nearly a month later, when he reported that the assistant keeper and family went to Matia. Lonholt had his own way of doing things. He reported the weather and passing ships on the right side of the page, and his own work came first on the left, breaking a seventeen-year tradition of how it was done. He also broke the record of reporting the work of his assistant. As far as the journal was concerned, the assistant did not exist. It is not surprising, then, that Clark had to hire another assistant for Lonholt if he went anywhere at all.

Postcard stamped 1913 of the Patos Island Lighthouse. George Lonholt was keeper in 1913.

Estelle Durgan and two of her daughters came to visit Mary on August 7. During their visit, Noel, Mary's son, fell and broke his arm. Lonholt tried unsuccessfully to signal boats for assistance; the following day, he went to Eastsound to call for a doctor. The *Guard* answered the call and took Dr. Reed to attend to the boy, then took Clark and his son to a hospital. At the end of the month, Roy Durgan came to visit his sister Mary and help them off for a two-week vacation. William Stark, then the assistant to Edward Durgan at Semiahmoo Harbor, came to fill in for Clark during his vacation.

William Harrower Stark had a long history with the Durgans and Clarks. He had visited at Patos Island beginning as early as November 1905, and for nearly a dozen times. He was at Blaine, then was third assistant at the Tillamook Rock Light in Oregon. Then he was back at Blaine again. There are many mentions of him being at Patos and helping out but never any sign of trouble. But Lonholt reported him to authorities for failing to start the fog signal at what Lonholt thought was the appropriate time. It is the first evidence in eighteen years on Patos of anyone being reported to the authorities for failing to do their duty.

On November 14, Mary Durgan Clark took sick and had to be taken to town for medical aid. Mr. Coutts of Sucia took her to Blaine in the *Sea Pigeon* and returned with William Stark, who took over when the keeper went to Portland the next day. Since the keeper had a new custom of reporting on seeing the East Cape and Turn Point lights and hearing their signals, Stark corrected the Lonholt terminology of East Cape to East Point. When Lonholt returned from Portland, he reported that he inspected the station and it was in good condition. Stark left the station on November 20, and the Clarks returned at the same time on the *Fox*, the substitute mailboat, with a sister-in-law to look after Mary. When he left for Blaine at noon on December 12, he got Daniel Clark to stand in for him.

Daniel Webster Clark was there again as acting keeper when his brother Noah A. Clark took his family to Semiahmoo to visit the Durgan family and do some Christmas shopping.[39] Then, early on Christmas eve morning of 1911, according to keeper Lonholt in his journal:

Asst. keepers [sic] *wife and sister and son came to dwelling 6:30 am bringing news of having been wrecked on N.E. point of island and that Mr. Clark was drowned while swimming from his disabled launch toward the shore for assistance. Acting asst. D. Clark and I searched the beach hoping to find Mr. Clark, but found no sign of him. Keeper left for East Sound to send telegrams 10 am and returned 4:30 pm. Revenue cutter Guard arrived at 7 pm to render assistance for the launch* Sea Pigeon *in which Mr. Clark and family was wrecked. Capt. Woolford of the Guard was partly blinded by rays of the light from the tower—and cam* [sic] *on a ledge of rock at the entrance to harbor. Side was falling and keepers assisted with putting timbers under stranded boat to keep her up right.* [sic] *At 5 am the Guard was afloat again and backed out in deep water and anchored in bay. Keeper of Semiamoo* [sic] *Harbor Light wife daughter* [Edward and Estelle, Clara and Estelle Durgan] *and Wm Stark arrived in launch Alaska Rover 7:20 pm on the 24th. Mr. Stark came to act assistant, but as Mr. Clark's brother was acting assistant already it was thought best to leave him take his brother's place. Moderate clear NW East Cape Light visible all night.*

Dec 25. Fresh NW wind blowing all day. Mr. Durgan, Mr. Stark, and I went out 9 am in launch Alaska Rover in hope of being able to pull the wrecked Sea Pigeon *of* [sic] *the rocks but failed on account of surf on beach and returned to harbor 10 am. later in the day the heavy seas broke up the* Sea Pigeon. *& Revenue Cutter Guard left islands for Friday Harbor at midnight. Fresh clear NW wind East Point Light visible all night.*

Dec 26. Daily Routine: Worked all day with wreck of Sea Pigeon *trying to get it above high-water mark in order to save the engine and equipment. Fresh SE wind East C* [crossed out] *Point Light visible all night.*

Dec 27. Daily Routine: Worked all day getting the Sea Pigeon *above high-water mark on beach. Revenue cutter* Arcata *called at the station inquiring about the launch Alaska Rover and Mr. Durgan and family. I reported all well to the Arcata and asked officer in charge to report the same to Inspector and asst. keeper C. Durgan of Semiamoo* [sic] *Harbor Light. Moderate SE overcast East Point Light visible all night*

Dec 28. Daily Routine: Mr. Durgan and family packing up household effects preparatory to leaving.

Dec 29…USS Heather *called at station 6 am left station at 12 noon with Mr. Durgan and family and Mr. Stark.*[40]

Living through a tragedy and then writing about it may be two different things. We know that a sister was in that boat with Mary and Noel all that bitterly cold, fateful night, and as was the custom at the time, no one said her name. Helene wrote in *The Light on the Island* that she was at the house when Mary arrived to report the drowning death of her husband. It has been assumed by others that the sister was Estelle. Yet the *Register of Visitors* shows that Edward and Estelle and their second and third daughters, Clara and Estelle, respectively, were with them when they arrived the following day. That leaves Helene, the fourth daughter, or one of the younger ones, Lulu or Thalia, to be in the boat overnight with Mary. Had it actually been one of the younger girls, Helene most likely would have said so. There was a special bond between Mary and Helene, and it shows up even beyond the pages of the book. After Edward Durgan died, Mary took Helene and Lulu into her home to finish high school and go to junior college. Their bonding could have grown that terrible night when the water began to swamp their disabled *Sea Pigeon.*

On the first of January 1912, Daniel Clark packed up to leave Patos Island and William H. Stark was back again as acting assistant. Lonholt claimed that he would have fired Daniel Clark for his poor performance had it not been for the unfortunate circumstances that brought him there. Yet, as the record shows, Lonholt worked hard to help the Clarks and the Durgans. But he did not like Stark. One piece of equipment after another developed problems and required attention. The torch that was used to start the engine for the fog signal didn't work, and the threads in one of the vaporizing tubes was broken. The clockwork, which never was reported as a problem before, quit working, and the lens had to be turned by hand. And the emergency lens had to be used while the vapor light was down, and then it broke, too. The spare emergency lens also broke down, and Stark reported taking pieces of one to fix the other. When the *Manzanita* came to pick up Mary Clark's household effects, Stark asked for a mission to go to Blaine with the *Manzanita* to pick up some furniture and have them bring him back the following day. Lonholt agreed to let him go.

While Stark was gone, Lonholt cleaned out the coal locker and wheeled fifteen barrows of coal and threw them overboard, claiming they were unfit for use. He failed to dry out the coal, as had been the custom. He removed the broken heater from the watch room and replaced it with the heater from the assistant's living quarters. As it was early February, the assistant must have been half frozen from staying in his room without any heat. Lonholt wrote in the journal that the assistant wished he could purchase a heater for his room. When Clarence Durgan came on the *Alaska Rover*, Stark returned to Blaine with him and came back on the *Fox* the next day, having ordered some furniture. The *Fox* brought his order on March 18. He had gone a month and a half without a heater and, since his arrival on January 1, without furniture. When the mail boat arrived with mail on April 11, the keeper wrote, "this is the first time in 13th day [*sic*] someone aught [*sic*] to report it to the Post Office Headquarters as we are suppose [*sic*] to receive mail 3 times per week." In spite of having just complained about it in the journal, he took that very boat to Bellingham. While he was gone, Stark wrote in the journal that the keeper had left for Blaine "to see his girl. Seems to be deeply in love." The keeper did not return for six days, and then without a girl. The facts of the case are interesting. He left North Bellingham on the regular run three days after he arrived, and when it stopped at South Bellingham, he got off just as the boat was departing. Whether he was having second thoughts about giving up on the girl is unknown. At any rate, he had to wait another three days to get back to Patos, still without the girl. From then on, Stark and Lonholt did their best to avoid each other. When one arrived, the other left shortly thereafter.

On August 2, the assistant wrote: "Keeper handed me WH Stark a letter from Inspector as regards to light. Keeper acting very strangely. Afterward stealing assist gas boat is leaving station. Put flag up for help or to get boat in so as to send report to Inspector at 12 noon." He went on to complete the journal daily and did work around the station, including fixing the vapor light ready for lighting and reporting each day that the keeper had not yet returned. Captain Newcombe of the Canadian fishery protection tug *William*

Jolliffe answered his signal of distress, and Stark reported the situation and gave him the letter to the inspector to mail. Newcombe apparently informed Inspector Henry Beck of Portland what had happened. On August 4, Stark again reported that the keeper had not returned, and then at 11:00 a.m. a tender arrived with the inspector. W.H. Stark was relieved by assistant Guy C. Martin. Lonholt tested the fog signal and recorded that it was in good order. The emergency lamps were all right. And he "[Lonholt] accidentally broke." It seems that any broken equipment was blamed on Stark, yet if he broke something, once Stark was gone, it was an accident. The newspapers reported that Stark had gone mad and the keeper feared for his life and so had to escape. While history has accepted that story, after reading the journal, we have our doubts. On December 19, just four and a half months after Stark's removal, the inspector came and found "neither the light and fog signal machinery, stove rooms nor the dwellings were as neat, clean and shipshape as they should have been. The keeper was instructed that conditions in this respect must be improved. Also, he must pay close attention to instructions from the office and observe them strictly. Henry L. Beck, Inspector." It was the first bad inspection Patos Island Station had in its nineteen years of existence! From that day forward until he left near the end of the year in 1922, he had only one good inspection, no excellent inspections and all of the rest were only satisfactory. On December 25, failing to mention it was Christmas Day, Lonholt reported that Mr. Hicks, assistant at Turn Point Light, came to relieve Guy Martin, who was going to Turn Point.

From the poor inspection forward, Lonholt never mentioned whether the East Point or Turn Point Light was visible or whether he heard their foghorn. Apparently, he was told that he was not responsible for reporting on them, whether he had ever been or ever thought he was. He failed to mention any boat travel that passed, except occasional mention of the government boats, yet from the beginning this had always been a part of the report. In fact, he wrote very little at all, made a lot of ditto marks and said not a word about any social visits or even about World War I, when the navy took control of all government lighthouses. Were it not for other sources, we wouldn't know that in 1914 excursion boats began taking people to Patos Island. Between July 12 and August 30, five steamers brought 149 people to visit the lighthouse. The following year, beginning on May 29 and through August 15, they brought 259 people on seven boats.[41] Yet, Lonholt seemed to be at his best when there was an emergency. He was cited four times for saving lives and property. First, he helped repair the launch *Meteor* and cared for its five occupants until it could travel again. Next, he assisted the yacht

Postcard of the *San Juan II* delivering mail to Patos, 1915. *Photograph by Louis Borchers, Turn Point Lightkeeper.*

Aquilla, which was disabled, and furnished shelter and care for its occupants until the engine was repaired. He went to the aid of the *Verona* of Seattle when it was overtaken by a storm and cared for its ten passengers for two days in the keeper's residence until the storm abated. And, finally, the *Meteor* ran into trouble again, and he kept the captain, engineer and a wife and two children until a launch came to tow the boat to Anacortes. Other assistants who served under Lonholt are William H. Taylor; a Mr. Wilson and his wife, Mary; Daniel Webster and his wife, Katherine, and their children William and Katherine Clark; and, finally, Hans F. Jensen.

George Lonholt, for all we know about him, still is somewhat of a mystery. He emigrated from Denmark in 1896, and in the 1900 census, he was serving on the *C.P. Patterson*, a naval vessel. In 1904, he was first assistant at Lincoln Rock Lighthouse in Alaska. By 1905, he was keeper of the Five Finger Islands Lighthouse in southeast Alaska, and he had a short stay at Ediz Hook, Port Angeles, Washington, in 1909. Then he spent two years at Semiahmoo Lighthouse near Blaine, Washington, before coming to Patos in 1911. He went back to Semiahmoo after he left Patos on December 7, 1922, and was there when it was automated in 1939. All of these lighthouses where he served, except Patos, have since been destroyed or replaced. He retired to a boardinghouse in Ferndale, Washington. Whether or not he tried to woo a girl in Bellingham, we do not know, except for William Stark's words written in the journal and Lonholt's extra three days of absence when he walked off the boat that was ready to depart South Bellingham. He was, however, a lifelong bachelor, which may have been a truly sore spot in his character. The biggest improvements during his time at Patos were the installation of the telephone in 1919 and a wharf in 1920. These improvements have not survived to this day. And the biggest stories—World War I and all the visitation by tourists—were never even mentioned in Lonholt's journal.

3

THE NINETEEN TWENTIES
AND THIRTIES

Patos Visitation and the Great Depression

O wen H. Wayson arrived on Patos on February 8, 1923, as assistant keeper, coming from Cape Flattery Light Station. N. Kroger left on August 2, 1923. When he arrived is not reported. George Lonholt did not say who his successor was when he left in December 1922, and the person failed to identify himself in any of our sources. The handwriting in the journal definitely changed, but the information given was even more sparse.[42] On the days the *Tulip King* brought mail, the only other information given was weather, and some days there were no entries at all. There were a number of assistants in rapid succession during this period, including J.W. Mead from September to November 1923, Charles V. Rosseau (November 1923 to January 2, 1924), H. Peterson (January 10, 1924) and John B. Bray (June 10, 1924). Just from handwriting, we think that Hans F. Jensen replaced Lonholt in December 1922 and stayed until March 21, 1928, when Criss C. Waters and his wife, Estelle, came. Waters was married to Durgan's third daughter, and in her book, Helene said, "Why, Criss was the best-looking boy I'd ever seen." Both Jensen and Waters had been to Patos earlier as assistants, and perhaps they were used to training new recruits. In January 1927, Jensen reported making a mast for the radio and putting the radio up. And in December 1929, Criss Waters had the telephone poles removed, as they were no longer necessary.

The implementation of the radio was the most significant event in the history of the lighthouse. Even the 1908 tower and fourth-order Fresnel lens did not match the importance of the radio. As Jim Gibbs put it: "The nostalgic sight of a light tower lifting its massive masonry will one day be reduced to a role of memory, and memory is fragile stuff. The modern radio-beacon is far greater insurance against disaster at sea than the most powerful beam of light ever flashed." And: "Remarkable new navigation devices—radio, radar—are capable of seeing through the thickest and nastiest of weather. Snow, rain, sleet, fog, the external enemies of the light and the foghorn, need no longer be of major concern to those who do business in great waters." As a beam of invisible light, the radio beacon uses Morse code as a signal that can be read by anyone with a radio receiver. The radio on Patos was used as a triangulation for seafarers. Either Point Wilson, Smith Island and Patos Island were in the first set of three in the northwestern Salish Sea, or later, Smith Island, Burrows Island and Patos Island. Each gave their Morse code signal in a series of ten minutes, one signal a minute, and then the next and finally the last, each with their unique signal, and followed by an identical thirty-minute period of signals. Whether this radio-beacon signaling began in 1927, as the journal appears to indicate, or 1936, as reported by O.J. Lougheed, is unknown at this time. But, whenever it happened, there was now a third important work item in addition to watching the light and the foghorn: watching the radio.

Patos has had a reputation for being a hideout for rum-running and other illicit activities, primarily because it is close to Canada, where all the illegal activity was allegedly from, far from any other island in the lower forty-eight states.[43] Patos has two bays in which to hide: one on the west end, known as Active Cove and well within the purview of the keepers; and one on the east end, originally called Blanchard's Cove but today identified as Toe Point. The east one is fairly secure. A number of caves are reported to be there; finding them depends on the cycle of tides. Finally, Patos Island is heavily forested. One could easily hide among the trees. In the mid- to late 1800s, the illicit trade in Chinese workers and opium and the shipment of wool from Canada to elude tariffs were the main issues. During Prohibition, it was alcohol.[44] According to Jim Gibbs, "Patos Island was a key violation area in prohibition days and much illegal whiskey was moved across the border as the blacked rum-runners utilized the light at Patos for guidance." Today, the issues are undocumented workers and street drugs. In *The Light on the Island*, Helene Glidden has tales of such illicit events, including the discovery of opium under the floorboards of

Mr. Blanchard's cabin on the east end of Patos just off Blanchard Cove. If such events occurred, they either were unnoticed by the keepers, as the book claims, or at least unreported by them. On February 9, 1925, keeper Jensen noted in the journal that a "U.S. Rum Chaser boat #68" called at the island. That's it. That's the extent of discussion on Prohibition and smuggling booze in from Canada. The name Blanchard, however, comes up over and over, but not in association with smuggling.

Since the lighthouse was built, the keepers depended on Blanchard for a lot of things, but primarily for rides from place to place and hauling various things, including livestock and household goods. He is reported in the journals as being a resident of Sucia. Yet, in the 1910 census, he shows up as living on Patos, which was reserved by the government for the light station. Never is Blanchard given a first name, and no personal information is given about him, but he seems to have been held in high regard. Helene Glidden referred to him as a historian, and she had Indian Joe showing up to ask the keeper to go to Bellingham when Blanchard was very sick in the hospital. Interestingly, there is a town on the mainland south of Bellingham named Blanchard. A road on Orcas that leads northwest toward Patos is also named Blanchard. And, oddly enough, a Farwell Blanchard Jr. shows up in 1931 in the *Register of Visitors*, and several Blanchards arrive in 1936, 1937 and 1938, all with an address of Pasadena, California. Sometimes, they signed the *Register of Visitors* in the company of the Gibson family of North Beach Inn on Orcas Island. Whether or not these persons are relatives is unknown.

Tourism in the area began to be prominent in 1914, and it continued to be a major business until the war heated up in Europe in 1938. Just how many visitors Patos Island had during that time has not been counted, but we do know that tour boats checked in at the major resorts in the San Juan Islands, Lummi Island, Seattle, Bellingham, Birch Bay and Blaine to pick up guests and take them touring to Patos for the day. One of the local tour boats was the *Tulip King* of Sucia Island. Captain William Harrison Harnden, owner and builder, started carrying mail in the *Tulip King* to Patos in 1922, and among other chores, his boat picked up tourists on Orcas and took them to Patos. James T. Geoghegan, Eastsound photographer, along with his three sons, took the *Tulip King*, and he gave us a good photographic record of the event. Harnden also served as relief lighthouse keeper, especially in the winters. His granddaughter, Shirley Guilford, recalled that her grandmother using hot-water bottles to warm the bed for her at night. She said it was very cold in winter in the keepers' quarters.[45]

Above: The *Tulip King* (1920s–1940s), owned and operated by William Harrison Harnden. *Watercolor by McLaren.*

Left: The *Tulip King* and owner Harnden served the keepers as shuttle and relief keeper.

The highest period of visitation was during the Great Depression, when traveling from abroad to the United States was quite affordable. The bulk of visitors were Canadians. On one day, July 21, 1933, 80 people visited. That year and the next, people came from Holland, Spain, Germany, Argentina, Scotland, England, Norway and India. Nearly every state in the United States had at least 1 person visit Patos. By August 1938, when the war began in Europe, there were only 220 visitors the entire year.

Let's go back to 1928, when Criss Waters was keeper and William J. Tillewine was his assistant. They planned for visitors, putting up ladders for times when the water was low and signs to show visitors which way to go. They regularly reported visitors, whereas the earlier keepers reported only those they knew.[46] We learn from them that the YMCA Camp Orkila regularly made visits to Patos with its campers. They usually stayed only an hour or two, but they came so frequently that they must have felt welcome. During the same time, the keeper had to row to Sucia to get help to get his sick assistant to the hospital. Although this left him shorthanded, he still welcomed visitors and showed them around. The *Tulip King* made calls and attended to getting folks to the doctor or hospital and even brought parts for the lighthouse equipment. In December, the *Tulip King* arrived with mail, supplies and two goats!

The *Tulip King* ran visitors from resorts to Patos Island, and the photographer, Corbett, was one of them.

J.T. Geoghegan, Orcas Island photographer, took sons Jimmy, Richard and Harold aboard the *Tulip King* to Patos Island.

The Geoghegan family waits in the shade of Active Cove for the *Tulip King*, just outside the harbor.

The reason for the lighthouse was not to entertain visitors but to serve as an aid to navigation. On an October evening in 1930, in the fog and haze, the *Henry Grove* of New York ran onto a reef; it took the help of others for the keepers to get it off two days later. In April 1931, there was a change of keepers; Orlo E. Hayward took over from Criss Waters, and Forest M. Christner was his assistant, in place of Tillewine. Again, a year later, the October fog set in, and the *Elizabeth Drew* of Seattle struck a reef on the east end of Patos, punching a hole in its hull. The owner temporarily patched the hull and went to Bellingham for more substantial repairs.[47] But before leaving, he arranged with Hayward to leave his brother Gay Railton in the keeper's care until he could return with a safe vessel to claim him. Two days later, Hayward severely injured his back trying to raise the anchor mooring for his launch. The *Heather* came and took him to the Marine Hospital in Port Townsend. The following day, a Coast Guard vessel arrived with Henry Hill as relief keeper, attending to the usual duties plus the care of Gay Railton. In Hayward's absence, his cow needed to be barged to Orcas for veterinary treatment, and the inspection of the station occurred. On the ninth day, Frederick Railton returned for his brother, who, no doubt, had quite a tale to tell of life on Patos Island! Meanwhile, Hayward's injuries continued to require treatment, and he did not return to the station until December 15.

A year later, the story was about the same in terms of the health of the keepers. Hayward again injured his back, as did Christner. Both keeper and assistant had long bouts of back injuries but still managed to get up new visitors' signposts and hang dock ladders, and they had everything painted and fresh for the visitor season. But on July 29, 1932, the keeper was returning from Eastsound, where he had gone for mail and supplies, and he saw the *Hedgeland* stranded on Parker Reef. An eighty-foot diesel freight boat, it was headed for Fox Island, Alaska. Two Coast Guard vessels were there to render assistance, so, instead of joining in the rescue, Hayward determined to just notify the office. No doubt his back reminded him that he would be of little help under the circumstances. Machinists called to overhaul the light and the fog signal, and carpenters came to build new water tanks. The keeper was moved to Cape Blanco on the Oregon coast.

OCTOBER 9, 1933, EDMUND N. Cadwell and his wife left Cape Blanco to take up duty at Patos Island. Unlike any other previous keeper, Cadwell began by signing his name at the bottom of every page in the journal, as if to certify his work. He made a "thorough checking of Station Equipment found items practically okay." When assistant Forest M. Christner left on annual leave, on December 1, Cadwell reported in the journal that he "left his quarters very dirty."[48] Relief assistant Froggatt cleaned the dirty quarters before occupying them. Froggatt himself fell into disfavor on the twelfth when he left the sea cock open and swamped but did not sink the launch. Then, on December 19, a southwest storm of "syclonice force" [*sic*] blew down trees and fences and did other damage on the island." The following day, Cadwell wrote that there was "terriffic [sic] force again" and the lantern was badly shaking at lighting up time and he "had to brace doors in Signal to keep them from blowing in, water beating in through windows and doors and many trees fell again today. Boat house doors washed away & other damage." It was a two-week storm in all, and on the fifth day of it, Mr. Harnden brought the mail, the first they had in sixteen days, due to the launch being out of commission. And on December 31, Harnden called again with batteries and coil for the launch. The storm had abated, and most of the two inches of snow had melted. Cadwell fixed the launch and had it running after nineteen days. In his journal, he wrote: "A very stormy Dec. The end of the month and the end of the year E.N. Cadwell, Keeper."

Frank Dorrance (*left*) and Wallace Ervin. Dorrance was head keeper from 1938 to 1941. Wallace was there in 1935.

That is the last journal entry available for us to use to record the history of the island. One can't help but think that Harnden's two neighborly visits just to help out, plus the disastrous storm totally out of man's control, must have made an attitude adjustment on Cadwell. We don't know how long he stayed on Patos, but Christner left the following year and Richmond E. Umdenstock took his place. Others who served in the 1930s were Wallace Ervin, Fred H. Walker and Frank W. Dorrance, who was keeper.

Edwin George Clements, assistant, and his wife, Bessie, came from the Turn Point Light to Patos in 1939. They were generally a very happy couple; however, they were perturbed that it took so long to get another transfer to Smith Island, which they expected to be their last assignment before retirement. The Lighthouse Service and the Coast Guard merged that year, and with the change, personnel had to be assigned and take time to learn their new positions. Finally, the transfer to Smith Island came. But on the Clements' arrival, a storm raged, and Clements took another man's assignment to relight the lamp on Minor Spit. It was his last assignment. He drowned that night, December 29, 1939.[49]

4

THE NINETEEN FORTIES

World War II

There is no question but that the Civilian Conservation Corps (CCC), created in 1933, not only helped the country get through the grips of the Great Depression but also equipped the nation's young men to become the terrific fighting force that dealt successfully with World War II. One of the earlier CCC camps, and the first in the state of Washington, was Camp Moran in Moran State Park, Orcas Island, just south of Patos. Ellsworth Storey was the young Seattle architect who joined the U.S. Park Service to design the sandstone rock and log structures built there by the CCC. The most famous structure still standing today is the Observation Tower on Mount Constitution. From the tower, completed in 1936, one can see the mainland mountains of the Cascade Range from Mount Baker to Mount Rainer and the islands offshore in between. Most likely, Ellsworth Storey first saw the Patos Light sending out its signal into the night from the top of this tower. He and his wife climbed the Patos Lighthouse tower and saw the source of that light on August 23, 1939. In the years to come, Patos would have another tower; it, too, would be an observation one, but not for fires or visitors. This tower was built for looking for enemy planes, ships, submarines and incendiary balloons.

Our World War II story comes from two sources, June Burn and Rupert Hagan. June Burn was a young writer living on Waldron Island with her husband, Farrar. In the summer of 1946, she contracted with the *Seattle Post-Intelligencer* to write a travel log titled *100 Days in the San Juans*.[50] She and her husband traveled through what is now known as the Salish Sea in their boat,

Bob Kelton, photographer of the CCC construction of the tower on Mount Constitution, Orcas Island, in 1935.

Watercolor postcard of the CCC tower by J. Boyd Ellis, Ellis Post Card Company, Arlington, Washington.

Rupert V. Hagan photographed this view of the lookout tower on Patos Island Light Station during World War II.

the *San Juanderer*, a surplus Coast Guard boat. On the thirteenth day of her one-hundred-day journey, her story "Lonesome Lighthouse Lads" was about Patos Island. Farrar served as the photographer for his wife's stories, and the photograph selected for publication was of the original keepers' quarters. She described the previous night before her writing day began: "We found the sweetest graveled beach and sheltered cove and sleeping plateau we've ever had in all our camping years. The beach fell away sharply so that our boat hadn't such an easy chance of going aground." She is describing Active Cove, Minnie's Beach, named for a keeper's wife who loved to skinny-dip, and the Washington State Parks campground of today. It is the same cove and beach that the Coast Salish used for thousands of years before the Burn family landed there. "It rained during the night, pat-pat-pat, right close above our heads on the canvas—a sweet sound when you know that everything is well covered against it."

The night before, after anchoring in the cove and rowing a skiff ashore, they walked up the trail to the light station. "Instead of the two families we expected to find, four young boys were stationed here." The one in charge was a twenty-six-year-old Native American from Oklahoma, and the youngest was a twenty-year-old from Stockport, Iowa. None of them had been there longer than three months (which they thought was too long!).

Keepers' residence as it appears in the 1930s, as photographed by James T. Geoghegan.

She reported that a Coast Guard cutter brought them supplies every week and that each man cooked for himself using the ninety-nine cents per day allowed him by regulation. For the general population during the war, there was rationing of many things, including food. One needed to have stamps to purchase many rationed items. But for these growing young men, no rationing existed. Here is their typical weekly grocery list:

> *2 pounds cocoa, 25 pounds white sugar, 5 pounds brown sugar, 2 jars berry jam, 7 loaves white bread, 4 pounds butter, 5 gallons fresh milk…6 dozen eggs, 5 pounds cheese, 10 pounds ice cream mix, 4 pounds hotcake flour, half a case each of peaches, pineapple, assorted fruit juices, peas, canned milk, fruit cocktail; 10 pounds apples, 5 pounds oranges, 3 pounds grapefruit, 3 heads lettuce, 3 pounds carrots, 5 pounds tomatoes, celery, 5 pounds onions, one cured ham, 5 pounds bacon, 6 pounds round steak, 5 pounds pork chops, 5 pounds beef roast, 5 pounds hamburger.*

June and Farrar were treated to a visit to the lighthouse and all of its equipment. June was especially impressed with the radio and the jargon the men used to communicate with each other. "Nan Mike Williams, Nan Mike Williams—Nan Nan Fox Dog—have you any traffic for us? Over." And the reply: "Nan Nan Fox Dog, Nan Nan Fox Dog—Nan Mike Williams—affirmative—Over." While she was there, she learned via radio that an old friend of theirs who had risen to the rank of rear admiral was retiring. "Well, well, visit far-away lighthouses and keep up with your neighbors," she quipped. It is true that many of the young men stationed on Patos during the war were not there very long, as their record shows in the Visitor's Register. See the list of names in the appendix for comparison with other years, when peacetime aid to navigation was the reason to be stationed on the island.

Rupert Hagan is our first-person source of what life was like on Patos during the war. Rupert took his turn cooking for himself and the others, until, collectively, they determined that Russell Slocombe was the best cook. From then on, he held that main responsibility. At first, they did not know that Russell was also the best card player. Before long, even with their minimal wagers, Slocombe had all the spare money on the island. Not to be deprived of his favorite sport, he came up with another scheme to help redistribute the wealth so that he could win it back again. He hired each of the others to do his chores. Con artist? Yes, but the others loved him for it.[51]

On a more serious note, each of the men had his assigned specialty, in addition to the divided-up chores. Hagan was a watchman. The watch tower was manned twenty-four hours a day, seven days a week, and each shift was four hours long. Hagan's shift was at night. They looked for enemy planes, ships, submarines and incendiary balloons. Patos Lighthouse was in a blackout mode most of the time as a precaution, except at times when the navy advised that it be lit to protect the shipping of vital wartime supplies between California and Alaska via the inland passage. One night, when the lighthouse was turned off, Hagan called radio watch that he had seen six red lights. A few days later, officials came from Base Seattle to interview him. They discovered that it had been an exceptionally clear sky that night and the lights seen were from the Vancouver, B.C. airport. Even for the shorter hour-long shifts, the nights in the watchtower in winter were especially cold. The troops took no time at all to build a heater inside the watch tower and had a more comfortable shift. They were, however, careful to feed the stove a little wood at a time to keep it from getting warm enough to induce sleep!

Another wartime element that Rupert captured is the conscripted sailboat. During the war, the military had the power to take for government purposes the vessels belonging to the public. The accompanying photo of a once privately owned sailboat altered to serve as a lighthouse tender is a primary example. One time, when coal was being unloaded to serve as fuel for the

Left: Photograph of Rupert V. Hagan doing kitchen duty at Patos Island during World War II.

Below: Russell Slocombe, best cook and card player at the Patos Island Light Station during the war.

equipment in the lighthouse, Rupert recalled that "the tramway hauled among other things coal, which we sacked and then put in the basement. We were so dirty afterwards, we jumped into the sound. It was so damn cold! We never did that again!"

During the war, all family life disappeared. There were no children, no gardens, no farm animals. It was a military base. "We got all of our food from the supply boat. Sometimes we pried oysters off the rocks. We had a small boat with a small engine to use for fishing in our spare time, if we were not painting buildings. We painted buildings so often we joked that the officer Ben Wilcox (who gave us our assignment) must have owned a paint store. We used to see Lummi fishing boats close to the island." While Patos had been a veritable crossroads or stopping place for many years, and a recent go-to place for excursions, during the war, it was isolated from the rest of the world. "We didn't get a lot of visitors, but I do remember the Boy Scouts coming once. We used to get mail once a week. The Commanding

Opposite, top: The lookout tower was only present on Patos Island during the war. Photograph by Rupert V. Hagan.

Opposite, bottom: Photograph by Rupert Hagan shows the lookout tower and three red and white radio towers, important during World War II.

Above: Conscripted private sailboat converted to a lighthouse tender during the war. *Photograph by Rupert V. Hagan, 1945.*

Officer Ed Larson drove the boat to the north side of Orcas Island, and then we would walk to Eastsound."

Since the U.S. Navy was in charge of Patos Light Station during the war, it took inventory of the property for government records. The inventory included photographs of each structure, giving us the best image of what the station looked like in wartime. Our first good photographs of the water tanks, the carpenter's shed and the coal shed come from this period, as do the photographs of the barn, the boathouse, the 1939 chief's house and our first view of the north side of the keeper's residence.[52]

The most insightful photographs, however, come at the end of World War II. The occasion was the visit by Lieutenant Commander Ben Wilcox to inspect, then muster out, the troops. Rupert said that they had no idea how bad the war in Europe and the Pacific had been; they were just glad to know it was over. But in spite of their joy, the occasion of the Wilcox visit was very somber.[53] The Coast Guard vessel that carried Wilcox had a deep draft that could not land at the shallower dock at Patos, so Wilcox had to be met and transported by the station's smaller boat into the dock. Ed Larson, the officer-in-charge of the light station, offered Wilcox a hand as the transfer occurred. Once on site, the men stood at attention while they were inspected. Fortunately, Rupert remembered the event and

Seattle National Archives
Pump, carpenter and coal house, April 1944

During the war, the U.S. Navy took an inventory of the structures. This is the pump house, carpenter's workshop and coal house. *Courtesy of the National Archives.*

In 1944, the navy took this photograph of the barn, built in 1893, but not in use during World War II. *Courtesy of the National Archives.*

The boathouse, one of the original buildings, was essentially much modified due to the many storms that caused significant damage. *Courtesy of the National Archives.*

The officer-in-charge's house, built by the Coast Guard in 1939, when it merged with the U.S. Light House Service. *Courtesy of the National Archives.*

Keepers' quarters, back view. To the left is the top of the tram from the beach or boathouse. *Courtesy of the National Archives.*

Officer-in-Charge Ed Larson offers a hand to Lieutenant Commander Ben Wilcox on the Coast Guard vessel. *Courtesy of the Coast Guard Museum Northwest.*

all those in the photograph. The *Register of Visitors* added other details. Seen in the photograph below are, from left to right: Russell S. Slocombe of Los Angeles, California; Rupert V. Hagan of Long Beach, California; Arthur B. Diamond of Provo, Utah; Orville A, Hudson of Westport, Oregon; Calvin Hill of Oakland, California; George A. De Jarnatt of The Dalles, Oregon; and Edward Larson of Seattle, Washington. Ben Wilcox faced the troops as Yeoman Burrows took notes. For these men, the war was over, and for many, they were going home.

Rupert remembered that "we didn't know how good we had it on Patos. My brother was at Guadalcanal [battle in the South Pacific in 1942–43 with thirty thousand soldiers killed]. We didn't know how bad it was until later." The people on Orcas viewed the circumstances differently. In addition to the rations that everyone dealt with, many of them worked under the cover of blackouts, manning lookouts and towers while keeping an eye out for the same things the men on Patos looked for: signs of the enemy. Even the Orcas Island High School students had a sense that something terrible

It's 1945, and the war is over. Lieutenant Commander Ben Wilcox inspects, then musters out, the troops. *Courtesy of the Coast Guard Museum Northwest.*

had been averted. Their yearbook conveys their experience of the war in these words: "Dedication: This 1946 edition of the Viking is dedicated to the United Nations and world peace." The yearbook then listed 112 names of the men who had served in the war, many of whom had been classmates and family members, and starred 2 names of men who had lost their lives during the conflict. Then, on senior sneak day, the class went to Patos Island to thank in person those who had served there.[54] While the role may dim in comparison to those who had experienced the Bataan Death March and the Battle of the Bulge, Orcasites were grateful, because they knew that the men of Patos Island had their backs. Their post, on the northernmost military station in the lower forty-eight, had a critical impact on those nationwide who feared enemy attack.

FOLLOWING THE ARMISTICE, PATOS Island Light Station quickly made a return to the family days. Ovidio "Blackie" A. Petris was the officer-in-charge, and he and his wife lived in the chief's house the Coast Guard had built in 1939. The others lived in the original keeper's residence built in 1893. One of those young single men was Donald E. Fox of Cincinnati, Ohio. Don Fox was a radio man, but, like everyone else, he had his chores. When he first arrived, he was assigned a turn at cooking. On his first try, he made biscuits. No one ate the biscuits. He gave them to the dog. But the dog wouldn't eat them, either. So, he threw them over onto the rocks below for the seagulls. Gulls will eat anything, right? A few days later, he looked over the bank; the biscuits were still there. Even the seagulls wouldn't eat Don's biscuits.[55] There was finally time for fishing, picnics and family get-togethers. Thankfully, Don captured them with his camera. One of those events was the gathering of keepers from Turn Point and East Point Lighthouses. Such gatherings occurred from the early days of lighthouses in this part of the world, and they were finally captured on camera here at Patos. The picnic was in the back, or the U-shaped, northerly portion of the residence, away from the southeasterly breeze.

Readers will recall that Criss C. Waters, keeper from 1928 to 1931, was married to Edward and Estelle Durgan's third daughter, also named Estelle, in 1922. During America's first year of World War II, the Waters were stationed at Ediz Hook Light Station, Port Angeles, Washington. Estelle Marceline Durgan Waters died there of a cerebral hemorrhage on September 13, 1942. She was forty-six years old.[56] They had been married only twenty years. Their son James C. was seventeen by then, and their

Right: Donald Fox, circa 1949. *Courtesy of the Orcas Island Historic Museum*.

Below: Don Fox was a radio man at the Patos Island Light Station in 1949.

Coasty with two little boys shows off his catch of a large ling cod. *Don Fox, photographer, 1949.*

Don Fox captures an impromptu picnic on the sidewalk behind the residences at Patos Island Light Station.

Don Fox photographs a picnic of keepers from Saturna Island's East Point and Stuart Island's Turn Point Light.

daughter Marie M. was fifteen. Estelle's mother, Estelle Angie Durgan, followed her daughter in death the very next year.

On a brighter note, on July 4, 1949, Mary Durgan Clark Coutts and William Ulysses Grant Coutts of Everett, Washington, signed the visitor's register. They were celebrating the holiday on Patos, a place that carried a lot of meaning for both of them.[57] After Noah Clark drowned, Mary and Billy Coutts married in 1913. He worked as a mechanic at the dock in Everett. He adopted Noel, Mary's son, and took in Helene and Lulu Durgan and raised their own daughter, Anita, and son Virgil. From this home base in Everett, Helene and Lulu finished high school, Helene attended community college and Lulu got a job as a telephone operator. Through his long years of friendship and service to the family, Billy Coutts had a very special place in the hearts of the Durgan family and those of us who follow Patos history as well.

5

THE NINETEEN FIFTIES

The Revitalization of Patos Light Station

The decade began with the Korean conflict. The end of World War II did not leave the Asian or Northwest Pacific part of the world in a stable or settled state. The Cold War between the Soviet Union and America was an amassing of weapons and, most significantly, an ideological conflict between communism and capitalism. While Russia and the United States were fiercely competitive, neither country wanted open war. At the same time, the ideological split became one of several reasons for the Korean conflict. Soviet military advisors supported North Korea, and United Nations and U.S. troops were involved in support of South Korea. Yet, there was no fear of enemy attack on the United States itself. It was a war that affected primarily the families of those soldiers fighting, but not the American public at large, in the way World War II was. For Patos, it meant no blackouts and no lookout towers; in short, no fear.

Alvah Schultz was the officer-in-charge from 1950 until 1954. He and his wife, Arlene, lived in the chief's house. There were navy trailers on the north side of the complex on Alden Point. All other persons lived in the original keepers' residence.[58] The Coast Guard didn't assign men with school-age families here, but the quarters might be divided up differently, according to the needs of those assigned there at the time. For example, Clarence "Tee" Titterington was living there with Bill LaVergne and Bill Bellhorn when he married Elaine. The two Bills got busy in their spare time fixing up nice living quarters for the new couple. This marriage gave Arlene Schultz some female company and helped build camaraderie among the troops.

Left to right: Bill LaVergne, Elaine and Tee Titterington and Bill Bellhorn, all stationed on Patos Island in 1953.

This aerial phtotograph of Patos Island Light Station was taken by the Coast Guard during the Korean War. *Courtesy of the Coast Guard Museum Northwest.*

There was lots of painting to be done when Clarence Titterington arrived. "If it didn't move, we painted it, and sometimes painted it even if it did move." This seemed to be the way to break in newcomers, until it was determined what they were good for. By the time Clarence left, he was second in command; so, apparently, he proved his worth. They used a twenty-five-foot gasoline-powered launch to go to Orcas Island for supplies. They were very happy when they got a diesel, because, at times, waves washed over the boat and drowned out the gasoline-powered engine. They would go to North Beach and tie on to a buoy and take a twelve-foot skiff in, then drive the officer-in-charge's car to Eastsound. Here, they bought groceries at Templin's and picked up the mail at the post office. Alvah Schultz kept a car parked near the beach on Orcas for a way of getting around on the island. He used it for the weekly visits to town and for vacations. Finally, when he retired, he moved to Eastsound for a while.

"It got very windy on the island." According to Clarence Titterington: "Once Elaine was at the door and had the screen door ripped right off the hinges and thrown against another building. Another time the plank sidewalk, built in three 18" sections side by side, had some sections ripped up and blown 15' away. When the radio was out, we would tie a rope to the railings then to the flag pole, then to the lighthouse and then hook our arms around the rope to be able to get to the lighthouse without being blown away." One Christmas Eve, they were starting out for Orcas in the launch, Elaine watching from the porch. The sea was very rough. Just outside the cove they went into a deep trough, then into another trough outside the cove, and waves came washing completely over them. Elaine said it looked like the boat had gone down. They came around the south side of Little Patos and back into Active Cove, something that could be accomplished only at a high tide. "Like surfing in a 25' boat. Quite a ride!" Thankfully, they were all alive, and they were grateful for a merry Christmas!

Years later, Elaine recalled life on Patos without memory of those difficult days.

> One can understand why our 1st year of married life was like a honeymoon, year-round, since we spent it on Patos Island. The beauty of watching the sun set cannot be described in words; for what words would you use to describe a beauty no artist has been able to capture in canvas. The Western sky was alive with fire dancing on the long fleecy clouds, and the setting sun cast a reflection on the water in the form of a golden ribbon which ended

at the doorway of our home. Many happy hours were spent this way until the sun would disappear below the surface and the fire in the sky would gradually burn out.

They found a body in 1952 or '53 that they thought had washed overboard somewhere around Nanaimo. Authorities from Bellingham came and got him, but they never learned who it was or how he came to be in the water. This, no doubt, served as an unpleasant reminder that living on an island and traveling over the water could be dangerous and demanded respect.

Bill LaVergne's first job was painting the red-and-white-striped pole antenna for the radio system. "I guess I passed that test," Bill said. "The longer I stayed on Patos, the more I enjoyed it." Patos Bill told his story for the *History Nook, Island's Sounder* published on November 1, 2017:

My duty shift was midnight to 8 a.m. Everyone else was in bed sound asleep, I went to bed at 8 a.m. Then I got up for lunch and got busy with chores all afternoon. We did a lot of painting, building new cement sidewalks as the wooden ones were pretty much ready to be retired. They sent us two Coast Guardsmen from Seattle to help gather sand and gravel to make the cement we needed. They took buckets down to the beach area with our skiff boat and brought the gravel back up to the mixer that sat next to the tram in front of our houses. Needless to say, it took quite a few trips to collect enough to make a batch of cement. It was a long summer task.

Our Island life was like living on a farm. We planted a large garden, raised chickens and had a few goats. We kept the Billy on Little Patos. Summer was also time to get some fishing in. We had family and friends that came to visit, and boaters who came to view the lighthouse. So, it was always a time looked forward to by us. One time a woman and her daughter came by, and they learned that the following day was my birthday. They returned to take me sailing, and fed me birthday cake. Birthdays were celebrated with a dinner of the birthday person's choice. It was just like a family get together at one of our houses.

One of our enjoyable things I looked forward to was our weekly runs over to Orcas Island to pick up the mail and buy groceries. That was good because we made friends there and it added to our not forgetting how to interact with people other than the six people on Patos.

Andy and Kathleen Ritchie, Canadian light keepers from East Point, Saturna, would visit in the summer.

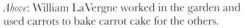
Above: William LaVergne worked in the garden and used carrots to bake carrot cake for the others.

Right: William (aka Patos Bill) LaVergne's official portrait in his Coast Guard uniform.

We often got called out for a rescue of people who had run their batteries down, etc. One time it was a group of Navy personnel. We helped them get running again. Did we ever love them having to ask the Coast Guard for help! I'm sure they never told anyone about that. We, of course, told everyone!

When TV came to the islands, we received a set and it sure was great for keeping up on what was going on in the world and to watch programs. Patos became the "Light In My Life." Patos Bill.[59]

Bill LaVergne also told us about the carrots he grew in the station's garden and the carrot cakes he made for the troops. So, to this day, when we celebrate the lighthouse's birthday, we do it with a carrot cake in honor of Bill's birthday, which is also in August. Bill serves as vice-president of the Keepers of the Patos Light and also the chairman of the flagpole committee. His goal is to erect the flagpole and be the first to raise the American flag again on Patos Island. Another Patos daughter, Dawn Alexander, serves on the board of directors of the Keepers of the Patos Light, and she has loaned us the Dale Nelson Collection, her father's set of slides to help learn about his time on the island.

Most of what we know about Dale Arlen Nelson's two tours of duty on Patos Island comes from his photographs and his letters to his wife, Darlene. When he first arrived in the winter of 1954, he described the island in a letter to her:

Right: Photograph of Dale Nelson, taken about 1954. Nelson served two terms on Patos (1954–56 and 1958–60). He loved it!

Below: Active Cove from Minnie's Beach. Dale Nelson's photo shows the dock for the lighthouse.

The island is big. It takes about 4 hours to walk around it. It's mostly woods that have never been touched. It's really beautiful. There is a little island right next to ours, it's called Little Patos. Between us is a cove where we tie our boats up. There are two other couples living here. They both have little kids, about 18 to 20 months old. They all seem very nice. The living quarters consist of a duplex and one house. We'd live in one side of the duplex which has 3 bedrooms, kitchen, living room, dining room, and a bathroom with a tub.

Nelson spent Christmas with a dinner at John and Marcia Weichert's in the chief's house. John was the officer-in-charge. Being included in the festivities was important to the young man, who missed his wife. And soon, if not already, he earned their deep respect and gratitude, as well as ours:

We really had some excitement here today. This morning I had the 6 to noon watch and at eight I went down to secure the light. As I opened the door to the tower, all I could see was smoke, so I turned on the fire alarm and tried to find the fire. It was up on the roof and had burned into the attic. We put it out in about a half hour. It left a big hole in the roof. I put a temporary patch on it for now. I guess if I hadn't gone into the tower the whole damn building would have burned down in a few more minutes.... We think it was a spark from the generators exhaust.[60]

Thankfully, they got the fire out in time to save the lighthouse. But another fire during his tenure was intentional. It was the destruction of the 1893 keepers' residence. The photographs of its demolition are difficult to see, and others who were there following the removal were very sad. Yet we must remember that the Coast Guardsmen were following orders and that, in that day, newer was better, smarter and up-to-date. Thankfully, two other lighthouses in San Juan County, the Turn Point on Stuart Island and the Lime Kiln on San Juan Island, still have their original keepers' residential duplexes. Both were designed by Carl Leick, the famous architect of the Thirteenth Lighthouse District.

At the time, those who had lived in the original residence were happy and proud of their new quarters. Here are some comparisons of their living situation: Darlene Nelson with a helper doing dishes in the original kitchen, compared to the new triplex modern and compact kitchen; the old living room at Christmastime in the original residence, compared to the modern new living room in the triplex; the original dining room in

Demolition of the original keepers' residence in 1958 was captured in a series of photographs that are heartbreaking.

Demolition of the keepers' residence was lauded as progress at the time but today is mourned by all.

When the keepers' residence was demolished, it was bulldozed over the bank and set on fire.

comparison to the modern new one with large windows and a view of Active Cove. The new structure was the finest quarters in the area and considered modern living in its day. The triplex, which later was subdivided even further to make more room for others, was the best place for Coast Guard families to live.

Patos Island Light Station changed in many ways while the Nelsons were there. Instead of travel always by watercraft, the island was visited most generally by helicopter. And they had their own truck to get around on the island and haul things, instead of always walking and carrying. They received new technology for the lighthouse, as well. There were three new Continental Red Seal Four Cylinder Diesel generators made in Muskegon, Michigan; two Ingersoll Rand air compressors for the fog signal; and new radio equipment. All of these changes were a result of the technology increase during the war. The brightest minds in the country had to come to its aid in the time of war, and the new knowledge and capability set the stage for upgrades in aids to navigation at Patos and other light stations around the country.

Another interesting phenomenon occurred while the Nelsons were there. Others, too, took a second tour of duty on Patos or stayed for a longer period.

Darlene Nelson (*left*) and helper washing dishes in the original keeper's kitchen—a comparison with that which follows.

The 1958 triplex kitchen is modern and compact.

A 1955 view of the living room of the original keeper's residence shows infant Dawn Nelson.

David (*left*) and Dale Nelson, wearing Coast Guard hats, frolic on the living-room carpet of the new triplex.

Dale Nelson's twenty-first birthday party in the original residence dining room, taken by Dale himself.

Darlene, David and Dawn in the new triplex dining room with Active Cove in the background.

This is the new triplex for the Coast Guard families. Photograph taken by John Christensen.

Dawn Nelson and the new sidewalk in front of the helicopter pad. The background is the triplex under construction.

A truck was assigned to Patos Island Light Station in the late 1950s.

Dale Nelson photographed the old engine to document it before installing the new engines. Note the hand crank.

New generators installed on Patos in 1958. Having hoist and truck made it easier to install heavy equipment.

Dale Nelson records the old radio equipment before they take it out and replace it with new.

The new radio equipment in the center room in the lighthouse on Patos in 1958.

William M. Crumrine (wife, Lou Ellen) was officer-in-charge from 1955 to 1958; Larry (and Carol) Geer took two terms (1955–57 and 1958–60); Ray (and Sharon) Henderson (1956–60); and Chet (and Cindy) De Wolfe (1956–62). The men must have enjoyed working together, and the wives and children got along, as well. So, they stayed until their children were of school age. Other changes occurred in the kitchens of Patos Island. The wives didn't store flour or cereal in sacks but bought smaller quantities in disposable paper bags or boxes. They didn't take all day preparing meals, since most foods came in cans, boxes or as frozen meals, especially TV dinners. And the new generators supplied enough electricity to power their new appliances, except, of course, when the fog signal sounded.

Diapers drying on the clothesline was a part of the scene at Patos Island Light Station in the second half of the 1950s. Larry and Carol Geer had two sons, Terry and Kenny.[61] When they purchased their own boat, they named it *Teriken*, after the boys. They took the *Teriken* to visit Saturna Island and the light keepers there. Dale and Darlene Nelson also had two children, a daughter, Dawn, and a son, David. Dawn Nelson and Terry Geer were the two oldest children and, so, were best pals, even playing outside in the winter. Dale hoped to raise David as a Coasty, as

The Geers visit the Crumrines. *Left to right*: Carol holding Terry Geer, Bill and Lou Ellen Crumrine, officer-in-charge, and Larry Geer.

Left to right: Larry, Terry (*in front*) and Carol Geer and David, Dawn (*in front*) and Darleen Nelson picnic on the beach on Active Cove.

Right: *Left to right*: Keith Haglund and Larry and Carol Geer on the Patos dock.

Below: Grandmother Lois (*left*) and Terry Geer petting the young deer, diapers on the line in the background.

Right: Dawn Nelson (*left*) and friend Terry Geer on the beach at Active Cove, Patos Island, circa 1959.

Below: Ray Henderson used the station boat to try to get others water-skiing. It didn't work.

Above: This is likely Doris holding Craig, and Joni and Debbie standing in front of their dad, Walter Dorethy.

Right: David Nelson as future Coasty in his dad's coat and hat. *Dale Nelson, photographer.*

seen in images of their playing around. The adults played, as well. On a hot day, Ray Henderson in the station's boat tried to pull others during water-skiing, which, with such a small motor, never happened. But they all had a good time playing in the cove and didn't mind the cool, fresh water. Walter and Doris Dorethy, along with their three children, Joni, Craig and Debbie, were also stationed at Patos during this period, and their children were likely playmates of the others.

Lucile McDonald, a journalist and historian, visited Patos Island Coast Guard Station in 1959, according to the Saltwater People Historical Society post of February 1, 2018. Dale Nelson took her to exposed sandstone outcrops to look for fossils. She reported that, a few weeks before her visit, Carol Geer had caught her hand in a washer; in a few minutes, a helicopter from Whidbey Island landed and took her to Oak Harbor, where she was flown to Seattle to the hospital. She was back before the day was over. On a more historical note, Lucile writes:

In 1858 Alden and his ship were in the service of the Boundary Commission. This was the vessel's last season in the Puget Sound area.

A part of the time a land party under James S. Lawson occupied a survey station on the eastern end of Patos Island. The steamship, meanwhile, made hydrographic studies along Canada's Saturna Island. Charts of that year labeled the Canadian Gulf Islands as part of the Washington Coast.

Alden's reconnaissance served for more than 100 years, except for some minor additions in 1891, when a formal survey was conducted.

This year the US Coast and Geodetic Survey is checking again, completing the resurvey of San Juan waters which began some years ago. Only the south end of Georgia Strait remains to be covered.

Two members of a survey crew moved to Patos Island 1 May to operate a short-range electronic-control station here in conjunction with another at Point Roberts. The survey ship HODGSON also is working in the area.

When the 1859 [sic ,1959] surveys are finished, tidal-current charts can be used for the entire San Juan Archipelago, an aid to small-boat navigation for which there have been many requests.[62]

6

THE NINETEEN SIXTIES AND EARLY SEVENTIES

Modern Amenities, Old-Time Storms and Automation

Harold Faust was the officer-in-charge, who, along with his wife, Helen, daughter, Kathy, and son, Mike, lived in the new triplex at the Patos Island Coast Guard Light Station. There were three other families assigned to the island, so there was adult company and plenty of playmates for the children. One of the other families was Norman and Judy Nolan, with Timmy and Tammy, their two children.[63] And there were often guests doing various chores for the station who were from Base Seattle. When the visitors arrived, they had separate quarters, but the wives took turns cooking for them, earning the per diem each man had coming, to add a little to their own table fare. The Base Seattle men loved coming to Patos, where, according to one report, "it was like going on vacation!" The wives loved it, too. They had extra money to purchase food and tried to out-do one another with their cooking. Their husbands must have loved it, as well!

There were also navy men working in the north sound and living in trailers on the north side of Alden Point. The Faust dog, Sandy, loved the navy guys, because they cooked steak nearly every night and always saved a bite for her. Sandy became so infatuated with the men that she would climb a tree and listen for their boat to be sure she was there to greet them when they arrived home. Yes, Sandy could climb trees, or at least the one down near the boat dock that the wind from the south had leaning at a considerable northward tilt. On one occasion, she got aboard the wing of a navy float plane, and it departed before she was discovered. The plane had to come back to return her home.

Kathy (*left*) and Mike Faust in front of the officer-in-charge's cottage. They chose to live in the new triplex.

Helen Faust (*left*) serves seven men from Base Seattle who have a temporary assignment on Patos.

Sandy, the Fausts' dog, with Active Cove in the background.

Sandy climbed this old fir tree with a lean produced by the southeast wind for a better view.

The Fausts had the bad luck of living on Patos during one of the worst storms in history, the notorious Columbus Day Storm, October 20, 1960. Harold said that the wind gusts were over one hundred miles per hour and the ice storm was so bad that they had to slide on their bellies, holding to the sides of the sidewalk and to one another to make it to the lighthouse, where they stayed for the duration. They had to be there to check on the light itself, make sure the fog signal sounded when necessary and, especially, to keep the radio beacon going. They had to keep the triangulation up with Smith Island lighthouse and Burrows Island lighthouse. They had the third three-minute shift. While this was always the most important duty, it was especially critical during the storm. They had no idea who might be caught out there in it. While they were engaged inside the lighthouse, the wives and children stayed in the basement of the 1939 chief's house, as they were afraid the triplex, only two years old, might not stand up to the wind. When the storm cleared and they assessed damages, ten or twelve madrona trees had completely uprooted down toward the dock. They cut up the trees and made the wood available to people who came there the following year to camp. Meanwhile, Orcas Island did not fare well, either. Hundreds of trees were down all over the island, and Moran State Park was hit exceptionally hard. To this day, the old folks here still talk about the terrible Columbus Day Storm.

One of the highlights of their life on Patos Island was the annual visits of the Santa Ship each Christmas. The children got special packages delivered directly from Santa, and Santa got his treats from the moms and dads, too! On January 6, 1961, the Fausts got a letter from Waldron Island's most famous resident:

Happy New Year to my neighbor lights-in-the-windows! All fall, from my tiny study here on a bluff almost due south of you I have watched and loved your lights.

At first there were three, now only two. What has become of your neighbor? Gone off on Christmas vacate on? I miss that light. I feel like swimming over with a dime to put under the pillow for the missing tooth in that row.

What do you set the big light by? I watch and watch and cannot be sure. Exactly sunrise and sunset by the book? (Which book, then?) My Westclox keeps such erratic time I never can be sure. And your light and Saturna's do not always come on or go off together. Perhaps you both light up according to fog or cloud around you?

Santa stops at Patos Island Light Station, bringing Christmas to the families on the island. *Harold Faust, photographer.*

You'll be surprised how fond of you I've grown. As if you were longtime and dear friends, or perhaps my children (for I am old). I wish you would get in your boat and come over to Study Beach, up the little mud steps cut into the bank, on around the salal trail to the Study. I live alone up here until our tank down at big cabin gets full of water. (We catch rain water off the roof of the main house, all same Burmuda, so vacate it till the tank is full so as to keep out tar and smoke. Of course we could build a filter but it is more fun this way, I in the Study, my husband in his Shop down in the scallop at Fishery Point on the chart). Thus we go away for the winter without any expense at all.

We have been to Patos two or three times hunting beautiful pebbles and once, fifteen years ago, camping over night beside that deep bay on the South side. (Oh, we had permission! We were writing a daily column about the islands for the PI that summer). Patos seems to us far away and romantic though I see you so clearly all day long and your lights all night long.

Do get in your boat and come sometime! If I am not at the Study I'll be down at Farrar's shop or somewhere temporarily. Come on in. I'll give you Alabama hot hoecake, butter and salal jam if I haven't eaten it all, in which case it will be merely wild blackberry jam. What fun, if I am working at the window, to happen to see a little boat put out from Patos, come straight across to Study beach; to hear the voices though I am deafish; to see you at my tiny door. Be careful; it is low.

Meanwhile keep happy. For, sight unseen, I love you. I love you as the only neighbor in sight; for the faithful light you keep; for the beautiful beaches and pebbles; for your lonely vigil off up there—the romance of it to us whatever it may seem to you as humdrummity!

Cordially, Mrs June Burn, via Coast Guard at Friday Harbor, for I do not know your address.[64]

Yes, she is the same June Burn who wrote about the "Lonesome Lighthouse Lads" in 1946. She also wrote *Living High: An Unconventional Autobiography* in 1941. June and Farrar Burn lived out their final years on Waldron Island, just south of Patos Island Lighthouse. When Harold and Helen got this letter, they had no idea who she was, but fortunately, they kept it, and we, today, are the beneficiaries.

Helen homeschooled their daughter, Kathy, so that she could pass her kindergarten test and stay on the island another year before starting to school. But their stay was cut short when Mike, their young son, had a confrontation with a lawn mower. The helicopter came and took him to the hospital. They had to remain close to the doctor; so ended their life on the island. Harold stayed with the Coast Guard, however, and retired with twenty-six years of service. And Mike's wounds healed thoroughly. He doesn't even have a limp!

JOHN AND DONNA CHRISTENSEN and their children, Susanne and Jeffery, lived in the chief's house from 1964 to 1967. The officer-in-charge, Patrick Newman, his wife, Sherry, and Diedrie, their daughter, lived there from 1965 to 1967. They preferred to live in the new triplex. Susanne took well to living on the island and participated in raising the garden. John loved for Susanne to go down to the lighthouse with him. And he liked to tease her about the frog in the Helene Glidden book being the ancestor of the frogs on the island and about the monkey in the tree. But, most of all, he liked to see her watching for vessels to stop at Patos. The reason she watched was because the Coasties always gave her a treat![65]

John gave the same care and attention to his work as he did to his family. He drew a floor plan of the lighthouse to show the location of the equipment when he was there. It shows the location of the three Continental diesel generators and the two Ingersoll Rand air compressors that ran off electricity

Right: Susanne, daughter of John and Donna Christensen, holds a squash or pumpkin from the Patos Island garden.

Below: Susanne Christensen looking for the arrival of a Coast Guard vessel. The men always brought her treats.

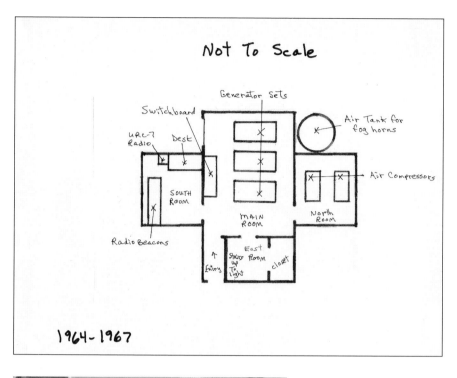

Above: Floor plan and location of equipment, drawn by John D. Christensen from his time on Patos, 1964–67.

Left: Continental diesel generators instruction manual, Patos Island Light Station. *Photographer, John D. Christensen.*

produced by the generators. The air compressors ran one at a time, filling the air pressure into a tank just outside the north room. Once it reached the right pressure for use on the foghorn, the compressor idled until the pressure dropped to a designated point then began filling the tank again. When the air compressor ran, the families usually did not have enough power left to operate their appliances. So, off with the TV programs!

In 1969, the first keeper's two daughters, the Mahler girls, also known as the "lighthouse girls," Frances and Margaret, signed in the visitor's register, as did someone who wrote, "Neil Armstrong was the first man to step foot on moon."[66] James M. Stephenson wrote that he was stationed on Patos in 1942, and John W. Weddal wrote that he was stationed there in 1943. And, yes, the visitor's register vouches for them. They were both there during World War II. Some people signed the register because they stood in line, and it was their turn. Others signed knowing their names were placed there for posterity. One such person was the one responsible for the automation. On June 24, 1974, Mr. and Mrs. Clifford D. Thresher closed the station, having completed the final assignment. Clifford left these words in the register: "One last thought before I go. Yesterday is already a dream, and tomorrow is only a vision. But each today well lived, makes every yesterday a dream of beauty, and every tomorrow a vision of hope. Automation is now in progress."

KEEPERS OF THE PATOS LIGHT

Thresher's Vision of Hope

For thirty-four years, the lighthouse held up to the violent storms, vandalism and lack of constant loving care. It operated automatically, the light shining at night, and the fog signal sounding when fog was indicated by the censors. But that failed, and the fog signal was removed. Not since 1892 had the island been so quiet. The long-dormant camas that over a century ago Coast Salish had harvested returned their blooms. Some clusters of flowers, like the California poppies, introduced by the families of Coast Guardsmen who lived on the island years ago, still bloomed. Campers came in summer, and Coast Salish still fished the waters. On a clear day, when Mount Baker could be seen to the northeast, the majestic lighthouse was photographed and painted. Some painters used oil, others watercolor, and still others found a sketch just enough to capture its silent beauty. It became the iconic image for postcards, telephone-book covers and a cover for a book about the lighthouse and its keepers. Always, most of all, it was adored.

BLM and State Parks began bringing parties of volunteers to cut back the vegetation, and in 2005, the Orcas Island Fire Department came to burn down the last of the remaining buildings, leaving only the lighthouse to hold forth on the island. It was about this time that BLMs' recreation specialist Nick Teague talked the Hudsons, Linda and David, and their friend Carla Chalker into organizing a group to help take care of the lighthouse. That group became the Keepers of the Patos Light, incorporated in 2007 as a nonprofit all-volunteer group. The following year,

Camas in bloom in the 1980s. By *Debra Madan, past president of the Orcas Island Historical Society.*

A sketch of Patos Island Lighthouse. *Mathew Villeneuve, University of Michigan, 2018.*

Patos Lighthouse in 1980s. Watercolor by Debra Madan, past president of the Orcas Island Historical Society, Eastsound, Washington.

BLM restored the lighthouse. The Keepers of the Patos Light is Clifford D. Thresher's vision of hope. Since that time, volunteers love to camp on the island and open the lighthouse to visitors. They sweep away the cobwebs, clean the floors and offer visitors a bit of history, including *The Light on the Island* by Helene Glidden. That book, which endeared all of us to the lighthouse, has been our reason to be. Other volunteers come with Sandy Evans, the retired nurse and master trailblazer, to maintain the campsites, trails and grounds around the lighthouse. They also clean the beaches. The San Juan County Ham Radio Operators come to and call lighthouses around the world and show visitors what it was like for the radio beacons to send out signals to help ships triangulate to determine their positions, regardless of the weather. It is this loving care that the lighthouse knew so many years ago that, now revived, keeps visitors coming and members joining the organization.

There are three things we are most grateful for. The first is Dale Nelson, who, in 1954, discovered the fire in the tower and succeeded in putting it out. We are fortunate that he wrote this story in his letters to his wife, and they have been preserved for us to discover. Had the lighthouse burned down, where would we be? The second is the revitalization of the lighthouse conducted by BLM in 2008. Had that not happened, we wonder whether the lighthouse would have survived to this day. Or would it have gone the way of the other buildings that once stood on the site? Thank you, BLM! The third thing we are grateful for is this: on June 7, 2011, the *Ruby Lily*, a fifty-foot fishing vessel carrying four thousand gallons of diesel fuel, ran aground on Patos, and the Coast Guard called the Islands Oil Spill Association (IOSA) to help them deal with it. The four very experienced volunteer responders dropped everything they had planned for the day and took off in the *Sea Goose*, arriving at the scene in short order. They surrounded the *Ruby Lily* with a boom to prevent the diesel from spreading. Once a barge could bring a fuel truck, they got 1,500 gallons of fuel off the ship. By that night, come high tide, the *Ruby Lily* was afloat again. They had saved the island and its marine life from the tragedy of an oil spill that could have ruined the coastline and the beach for many years to come. And they helped save the beautiful *Ruby Lily*, as well. Thank you, IOSA! To this day, hundreds of thousands of boats ply the waters of the San Juan Islands. They range from huge tankers

Greg Hancock (*left*) and Scott Miller use a ham radio to contact other lighthouses. *Photograph by Larry Gadallah, 2019.*

Scott Miller, ham radio operator, calls lighthouses from Patos Island, 2019. *Larry Gadallah, photographer.*

Greg Hancock (*left*) and Larry Gadallah call lighthouses from Patos Island, 2019. *Photograph by Scott Miller.*

Docent campsite, compliments of Washington State Parks, overlooks Active Cove, Patos Island, 2019. *Larry Gadallah, photographer.*

carrying oil and other cargo, ferries carrying us and all of our belongings and necessities, leisure boats of people who live for a day on the water, boats with our fishermen who depend on a day's catch for their livelihood and boats filled with visitors who come to enjoy the magnificent San Juan Islands and the Salish Sea. Each of these vessels depend on petroleum products, including the boats that moor on the two buoys in Active Cove. Let's hope that fire, neglect or oil spills never threaten the island, its fantastic marine life and its lighthouse again!

We, the Keepers of the Patos Light, are 150 members strong, meet quarterly in person or by phone and have a full complement of officers and a board of directors. We have standing committees and special committees, depending on the time and topic. We have raised money to restore a flagpole for this once military outpost and created historical exhibits to show our visitors how the lighthouse worked and who worked it. In addition, exhibits show the boats that connected the island and its inhabitants to the rest of the world. You can join us! You can volunteer to docent, do maintenance or support the work of others. We welcome you. We are the Keepers of the Patos Light at P.O. Box 1967, Eastsound, Washington, 98245.

PATOS ISLAND LIGHTHOUSE KEEPERS, ASSISTANTS AND OFFICERS-IN-CHARGE, 1893-1974

KEEPERS AND ASSISTANTS

Mahler, Harry D., Louise, Howard D., Francis L. and Katherine Margaret	**Keeper**	**1893–1903**
Durgan, Edward, Estelle, Mary, Clarence and Clara	Assistant	1893–94
Dunson, Joseph, Eleanor, Ray and Claude	Assistant	1894–98
Anderson, Gustaf	Assistant	1898–1900
Morgan, Albert A., Bertha, Clarence, Francis and Lucile	Assistant	1900–3
Morgan, Albert A., Bertha, Clarence, Francis, Lucile and Osmore	**Keeper**	**1903–5**
Pfaff, Edward, Lulu and Lucile	Assistant	1903–06
Durgan, Edward, Estelle, Clarence, Clara, Estelle, Roy, Cecil Rene, Helene and Lulu	**Keeper**	**1905–11**
Pettersen, Louis A. and Cheastie	Assistant	1906–9

Clark, Noah Alexander, Mary and Noel	Assistant	1909–11
Lonholt, George L.	**Keeper**	**1911–22**
Clark, Daniel Webster	Assistant	1911
Stark, William Harrower	Assistant	1912
Martin, Guy C.	Assistant	1912
Hicks, William H., and Mrs. Hicks	Assistant	1913–14
Taylor, William H.	Assistant	1915–18
Wilson, Mr., and Mary	Assistant	1918
Clark, Daniel Webster, Katherine, William and Katherine	Assistant	1918–21
Jensen, Hans F.	Assistant	1921
Jensen, Hans F.	**Keeper**	**1922–28**
Waters, Criss Curtis, and Estelle Marceline Durgan	Assistant	1923
Wayson, Owen H.	Assistant	1923
Mead, J.W.	Assistant	1923
Rousseau, Charles V.	Assistant	1923–24
Peterson, H.	Assistant	1924
Bray, John B.	Assistant	1924–25
Schuergers, Peter J.	Assistant	1925
Greene, Mr., and Ethel D.	Assistant	1925
Tillewine, William J. (Paterson, NJ)	Assistant	1927–30
Waters, Criss Curtis, Estelle Marceline Durgan, Jimmie C. and Marie M.	**Keeper**	**1928–31**
Jacobsen, Roy (Seattle, WA)	Assistant	1930
Christner, Forrest M. and Mrs. Christner	Assistant	1931–34
Hayward, Orlo E., and family	**Keeper**	**1931–33**
Cadwell, Edmund N., and Mrs. Cadwell	**Keeper**	**1933–**
Umdenstock, Richmond E.		1934–35
Ervin, Wallace	Assistant	1935

Walker, Fred H.	Assistant	1936–37
Dorrance, Frank W.	**Keeper**	**1938–41**
Clements, Edwin George, and Bessie	Assistant	1939
Beasley, DeMart C., and Emma J.	Assistant	1940
Kerney, Kenneth C., and Pauline E.	Assistant	1940
Gudgel and Flora "Nell"	Assistant	1940
Sheldon and Coral M.	Assistant	1941
Vincent, Clifford H. (Eastsound, WA)	Assistant	1941–42

Officers-In-Charge

Ringer, Glenn D.	S 1/c	Eagle Point, OR	1942
Geneghty, Jack	S 1/c	Pasadena, CA	1942
Sipe, Keith	S 1/c	Kalispell, MT	1942
Williams, Ralph J.	3rd C Qmstr.	Tulsa, OK	1942
Franklin, Benjamin H.		Seattle, WA	1942
Zent, Howard A.		Seattle, WA	1942
Stoy, Chuck A.		Seattle, WA	1942
Benton, Harry L., and Ethel		Seattle, WA	1942–43
Stephenson, James M.		Mill Valley, CA	1942
Weddal, John W.		Everett, WA	1943
Vanderwall, Robert		Portland, OR	1943
Keyes, Edward R., Jr.	S 2/c	Tacoma, WA	1943
Feltes, Daniel		Portland, OR	1943
Cromwell, Oliver H.		King City, OR	1943

Boyd, William O.	S 1/c	Denver, CO	1943
Straden, C.L.	S 2/c	Storm Lake, IA	1943
Sanregret, H.R.	CM 1/c	Bellingham, WA	1943
Zent, H.A.	MMM 1/c	Bellingham, WA	1943
Kelleen, George O.	RM 1/c	Seattle, WA	1943
Piper, James S.	S 1/c	Medford, MA	1943
Davenport, Paul	KT 1/c	Seattle, WA	1943
Bonitati, Patsy A.	S 1/c	Toronto, OH	1943
Diamond, Arthur B.	S 1/c	Provo, UT	1944–45
McClelland, Duncan W.	S 1/c	Los Angeles, CA	1944
Wood, Arnie L.		St. Louis, MO	1944
Paulsen, Paul K.	SC 3/c	Ketchikan, AK	1944
Adler, Horease N.	SK 2/c	Philadelphia, PA	1944
Hesson, Joan	S 1/c, (SPARS)	Philadelphia, PA	1944
Cushman, Floyd		Redwood, CA	1944
Twigger, Claude E.		Portland, OR	1944
Hagan, Rupert V.	S 1/c	Long Beach, CA	1945
Goff, Mr.			1945
Petrosky, Pete		PA	1945
Urkov, Johnny			1945
Shavere, R.J.	RT 1/c	Lewistown, MT	1945
Slocombe, Russell S. and Elsie E.	SC 1/c	Los Angeles, CA	1945

Hudson, Orville A.	S 1/c	Westport, OR	1945
De Jarnatt, George A.	S 1/c	The Dalles, OR	1945
Hill, Calvin		Oakland, CA	1945
Larson, Edward, and Elsie	**OIC**	**Seattle, WA**	**1945**
Holtkamp. Paul W.	S 1/c	Stockport, IA	1946–47
Kingsman, Norman H.	S 1/c	Seattle, WA	1946
Messer, Robert A., Gloria G., and Richard A.	**BM 1/c, OIC**	**St. Paul, MN**	**1946**
Rodriguez, Al W.	S 1/c	Dallas, TX	1946
Holmes, Fred, and Mrs. Holmes	MOMM 1/c	Eastsound, WA	1946
Pollie, John	BM 2/c	Boston, MA	1946
Watson, J.	MOMM 3/c	Los Angeles, CA	1946
Bolen, J.C.	Retired from USCG		1946
Butler, James E.	**MOMM 1/c, OIC**	**Burton, WA**	**1946–47**
Moody, William E.		Tulsa, OK	1946
Parkerson, Bill		East Chicago, IN	1946
Mattero, Joseph J.		San Francisco, CA	1946
Young, A.K.	S 1/c	Louisville, KY	1946
Petitt, Campbell R.	S 1/c	Los Angeles, CA	1946–47
Strack, Robert E., and Marjorie L.	S 1/c	Burlington, IA	1947

Petris, Ovidio "Blackie" A., and Mrs. Petris	S 1/c, OIC	San Francisco, CA	1947–48
Whitney, George R.	S1/c	Denver, CO	1947
Comer, James R., and Mrs. Comer	BM 1/c	Los Angeles, CA	1947
Henderson, James P., and Mrs. Henderson	S 1/c	Jefferson, OR	1947
Rohrer, Bob C.	S 2/c		1947
Lasper, R.A.			1948
Goodwin, E.C.			1948
Owens, J.W., Mrs. Owens and family			1948
Olson, Orville O.	BM 1/c		1948
Williams, Claude J., and Mrs. Williams			1949
Hoyle, R.M.			1949
Cowan, N.J.		Boise, ID	1949
Wilson, Howard V.			1949
Brown, N.		Boise, ID	1949
Fox, Donald E.		Cincinnati, OH	1949–50
Jackson, Robert L.	EM 3/c	Pacific Palisades, CA	1950
Turner, R.M.,and Mrs. Turner	1 3/c	Port Angeles, WA	1950
Lee, M.	BM1-AS		1950
Edgecomb, W.R.	FN	New Haven, CT	1950
Schultz, Alvah, and Arlene	OIC	Whidbey Island, WA	1950–54
Wood, J.E.	S N	Leavenworth, KS	1951
Ed (last name unknown)		Paris, KY	1952

Titterington, Clarence "Tee," and Elaine		Marysville, WA	1951–53
Bucko, Steve		Pittsburg, PA	1952
Bridgerman, George E.		Spokane, WA	1952
La Vergne, William T.		Tacoma, WA	1952–53
Bellhorn, Bill,		Detroit, MI	1952–53
Moe, Ron, wife and two boys		Portland, OR	195-
Reid, D.W.			1953
Johnson, Victor A.			1953
Salverson, George H., Dixie A. and George Jr.			1953–55
Baker, Lynn L.		Seattle, WA	1954
Hayes, W.P.	EN	San Diego, CA	1954–56
Hasenoehol, George J.	EN3		1954
Wiechert, John H., Marcia and Cynthia	**OIC**	**Nordland, WA**	**1954**
Nelson, Dale Arlen, Darlene and Dawn Angela	EN3		1954–56
Sands, Daniel P.	**BM1, OIC**		**1955**
O'Ferrell, L.D.	EM	Houston, TX	1955
Crumrine, William M., and Lou Ellen	**EN2, OIC**	**Port Orchard, WA**	**1955–58**
Geer, Larry H., Carol Patricia, Terry Lee and Kenneth	BM3	Berkley, CA	1955–57
Henderson, Raymond G., Sharon and Jay Sean	EN3		1956–60
Eaton, William E.			1956
DeWolfe, Chet E., Jr., wife and Cindy	BMB		1956–62

Dorethy, Walter L., Doris Ann, Joni Lynn, Craig Arthur and Debbie Ann		Macomb, IL	1957–58
Rolling, George H.		Astoria, OR	1958
Fisher, Robert A., and family		Bakersfield, CA	1958
Cartwright, A.E.	SN		1958
Yeadon, David B.			1958
Nelson, Dale Arlen, Darlene, Dawn Angela and David Alan	EN2		1958–60
Geer, Larry H., Carol Patricia, Terry Lee, Kenneth and Shadrack the dog	BM3	Berkley, CA	1958–60
Joy, William, Bev and Randy Scott		Joy, OK	1959–60
Powers, W. Fritz			1959
Alexander, L.S., Carolyn and Brian		Edmonds, WA	1960
Moore, Gary R., Lu Ella, Linda Christine, and Punky the dog		Seattle, WA	1960–61
Nolan, Norman, Judy, Timmy, Tammy Lyn and Susie the dog	BM3	Dryden, WA	1960–62
Faust, Harold P., Helen, Kathy, Mike and Sandy the dog	**BM1, OIC**	**Hayden Lake, ID**	**1960–63**
Holm, E.P., and Mrs.			1961
McKenna, Thomas T.	EN2	Keansburg, NJ	1961
Gile, Charlie E.		Seattle, WA	1962
Winson, Mr. and Mrs. Winson and two daughters		Everett, WA	1962–64
Denton, Jim, Diane, David and Darryl		Tacoma, WA	1962
Morrison, Gil			1963–64

Roberts, Ervin Stanley, and wife	**BM1, OIC**		**1963–65**
Gehring, George O., and Mrs. Gehring			1964
Smith, Don, Mrs. Smith and son			1964
Christensen, John D., Donna, Susanne and Jeffrey	EN1	Enumclaw, WA	1964–67
Moe, Ron, Mrs. Moe and two sons		Portland, OR	1964–67
Newman, Patrick E., Sherry and Diedrie	**OIC**		**1965–67**
Masters, Jim, Patsy, and Lesli			1966–67
Seidel, James T., Mrs. Seidel and son			1967–68
Hamilton, George E., Mrs. Hamilton and Kimberly Anne			1967–68
Moss, Alan P., Mrs. Moss and Jenna Fae			1967
Walker, Robert T., Mrs. Walker and son Etuck		Long Beach, CA	1968
Swisher, James F., III, Mrs. Swisher and son		Houston, TX	1966–69
Lane, Floyd L., and Mrs. Lane			1968–69
Conroy, Robert S. and Carol L.	BM3		1969–71
Buchanon, Larry L., Linda and Tammy Lynn	FN	Lompoc, CA	1969–70
Robinson, Dennis W., and family	EN2		1969–70
Chumley, Christopher	BM2		1969–70
Fife, C.E.	BM1		1970
Ames, K.D.	ET2		1970
Atwood, Thomas E., and Vicki			1970

Hurd, Lowell O., and Karen	BM2		1970
Fester, Steven E., and family	EN2	White Salmon, WA	1970–71
Senften, Dan D., and Deborah A.		Clackamas, OR	1971
Johnson, Terrence L., Carol L., Christina M. and Raymond C.	**BM1, OIC**	**Tillamook, OR**	**1971**
Carter, J.W., and Barbara	SN		1971
Miles, Keith W., wife and family	EN3		1972
Kinnan, John F., and family	**BM2, OIC**		**1971–73**
Boisleve, M.T., and family		Puyallup, WA	1973
Vaden, Charles F., and Mrs. Vaden	SN		1973
Lonholt, Terry L.		Wichita, KS	1973–74
Thresher, Clifford, D., and wife	**SN, OIC**	**Sedro Woolley, WA**	**1973–74**

NOTES

Chapter 1

1. Boswell, "Bison Bones Bolster Idea," *National Post*.
2. Barrie, et al. "Environmental Marine Geoscience 4."
3. Bellew, personal interview with Victoria Atkins, March 9, 2018.
4. Harry D. Mahler, *Journal of Light-station at Patos Island*, December 5, 1893–July 27, 1903.
5. "New Castle Island Marine Provincial Park." *Wikipedia*.
6. Villeneuve, "Helene Glidden and Her Lighthouse, 215–16.
7. "Wreck of the 'Rosenfeld,'" *Daily Alta California*; "Wreck of the John Rosenfeld," *Puget Sound Weekly Argus*, February 25, 1886; "Wreck of John Rosenfeld," *Washington Standard*, May 13, 1887.
8. *Lighthouse Friends*. East Point Lighthouse, Saturna Island, British Columbia.
9. "Many New Lighthouses," *Seattle Post-Intelligencer*.
10. Aliberti, *Lighthouses Northwest*.
11. "Office of U.S. Lighthouse Engineer," *Seattle Post-Intelligencer*.

Chapter 2

12. "Two More Appointments," *Seattle Post-Intelligencer*.
13. Harry D. Mahler, *Journal of the Light-station at Patos Island*, November 30, 1893.

14. Ibid., December 1–19, 1893.
15. Photograph of Rilling family, Orcas Island Historical Museum; Marriage Records, Harry D. Mahler and Louise Rilling, June 26, 1895, San Juan County Auditor, Washington State Archives.
16. "Sisters Recall Lighthouse," *Newport News Times*.
17. Harry D. Mahler, *Journal of the Light-station at Patos Island*, October 23, 1896.
18. "Sisters Recall Lighthouse," *Newport News Times*.
19. *Register of Visitors: Patos Island Light Station*, Orcas Island Historical Museum [various entries].
20. White, "My First Christmas."
21. "H.D. Mahler Gets Write Up," *San Juan Islander*, March 28, 1913.
22. Albert Morgan, *Journal of the Light-station at Patos Island*, July 27, 1903–December 7, 1905.
23. Ibid., September 27–29, 1903.
24. Ibid., December 25, 1903.
25. Ibid., July 4, 1904.
26. "University Marine Station," *San Juan Islander*.
27. Edward Durgan, *Journal of the Light-station at Patos Island*, December 7, 1905–February 22, 1911.
28. *Register of Visitors: Patos Island Light Station*.
29. Bureau of Vital Statistics, Death Index, Albert Arthur Morgan.
30. Glidden, *Light on the Island*.
31. Gibbs, *Sentinels of the North Pacific*.
32. Durgan, *Journal of the Light-station at Turn Point Stuart Island*.
33. "Farcical Test of Sunday Law," *San Juan Islander*.
34. Durgan, *Journal of the Light-station at Patos Island*, March 8, 1908.
35. Ibid., December 25–31, 1905.
36. Vinson, "Fourth Order Fresnel Lens," *Islands' Sounder*.
37. *Register of Visitors*, "Wm U G Coutts, Kenwood, California," July 28, 1907, 10.
38. George L. Lonholt, *Journal of the Light-station at Patos Island*, February 24, 1911–December 7, 1922; Vinson and Vinson, "George Louis Lonholt."
39. Vinson and Vinson, "Death of Noah Clark," *Islands' Sounder*.
40. "Heroic Act of Light Keeper," *San Juan Islander*.
41. *Register of Visitors: Patos Island Light Station*, 1914–39.

Chapter 3

42. Hans F. Jensen, *Journal of the Light-station at Patos Island*, December 8, 1922–March 21, 1928.

43. Gibbs, *Sentinels of the North Pacific*, 2; Lougheed, personal communication, 2017–19.

44. Gibbs, *West Coast Lighthouses*, 174.

45. Gilford, *Oral History*.

46. Criss C. Waters, *Journal of the Light-station at Patos Island*, March 23, 1928–April 26, 1931.

47. Orlo E. Hayward, *Journal of the Light-station at Patos Island*, April 27, 1931–October 8, 1933.

48. Edmund N. Cadwell, *Journal of the Light-station at Patos Island*, October 9–December 31, 1933.

49. Baldwin, "In Honor of a Forgotten Lighthouse Keeper."

Chapter 4

50. Burn, "Distance, Not Time Isolates Keepers," *Seattle Post-Intelligencer*.

51. Hagan, personal communication with Edrie Vinson.

52. National Archives and Records Administration, Seattle.

53. Coast Guard Museum, Northwest; *Register of Visitors: Patos Island Light Station*, September 9, 1945, 177.

54. *Viking*, 1946.

55. Lorenz, "Don Fox, 1947–48," *Islands' Sounder*.

56. Certificate of Death, Estelle Marceline Waters, September 13, 1942, Division of Vital Statistics. Washington State Department of Health; Index to Marriage Records, Snohomish County, Washington, 77; Sixteenth Census of the United States 1940, Ediz Hook Lighthouse.

57. *Register of Visitors: Patos Island Light Station*, July 4, 1949, 202.

Chapter 5

58. Titterington, personal communication with Carla Chalker, May 15, 2009.

59. LaVergne, "Patos Bill," *Islands' Sounder*; LaVergne, personal communication.

60. Dawn Alexander, Dale Nelson's personal communication with authors and photographic collection; Vinson, "Dale Arlen Nelson," *Islands' Sounder*.

61. Geer, photographic collection of Larry & Carol Geer and personal communication with authors.

62. "With McDonald at Patos Island Light Station," *Saltwater People Historical Society*.

Chapter 6

63. Faust and Faust, photographs and personal communication; Aberle, "Life and Times of a Former Patos Island Lighthouse Keeper," *Pacific Boating News*; Vinson, "Harold Faust," *Islands Sounder*.

64. Burn, personal correspondence with Patos Lighthouse personnel.

65. Christensen, personal communication and sharing collection with authors, 2017–19.

66. *Register of Visitors: Patos Island Light Station,* July 30, 1969, 272; August 14–15, 1969, 273; June 24, 1974, 285.

BIBLIOGRAPHY

Books, Articles and Personal Communications

Aberle, Mark. "The Life and Times of a Former Patos Island Lighthouse Keeper." *Pacific Northwest Boating News*, August 31, 2016.

Alexander, Dawn. "For 100 Years, a Guiding Light." *Islands' Sounder*, March 4, 2009.

———. Personal communication with the authors. Loan of photographs and personal collection of Dale Nelson. 2017–19.

Aliberti, Ray. *Lighthouses Northwest: The Designs of Carl Leick*. Self-published. *Daily Alta California*, n.d.

Anacortes Reporter. "Coast Guard's Skill Not All Nautical." July 8, 1964.

Armstrong, Colleen Smith. "The Little Lighthouse That Could." *Islands' Sounder*, March 3, 2010.

Baldwin, Debra. "In Honor of a Forgotten Lighthouse Keeper—Edwin G. Clements." *Lighthouse Digest* (May/June 2016).

Barrie, J. Vaughn, et al. "Environmental Marine Geoscience 4: Georgia Basin: Seabed Features and Marine Geohazards." *Geological Survey of Canada, Institute of Ocean Sciences*. Sidney, B.C.: circa 2004.

Bellew, Timothy. Notes from personal interview with Victoria Atkins. Northwest Indian College. March 9, 2018.

Boswell, Randy. "Bison Bones Bolster Idea Ice Age Seafarers First to Americas." *National Post*, March 24, 2008.

Bradley, Claudia. "Lighthouse Preservation Inspired by Classic Book." *Islands' Sounder*, December 12, 2007.

Bureau of Vital Statistics. Death Index. Albert Arthur Morgan. November 6, 1918. Washington State Board of Health.

Burn, June. "Distance, Not Time Isolates Keepers." *Seattle Post-Intelligencer*, July 1946.

———. Personal correspondence with Patos Lighthouse Personnel. January 6, 1961.

Cadwell, Edmund N. *Journal of the Light-station at Patos Island*, October 9– December 31, 1933.

Christensen, John. Personal communication and loan from collection. 2017–19.

Coast Guard Museum Northwest. Seattle, Washington.

Daily Alta California. "The Wreck of the 'Rosenfeld.'" February 22, 1886.

Edward Durgan. *Journal of the Light-station at Patos Island*, December 7, 1905– February 22, 1911.

———. *Journal of the Light-station at Turn Point Stuart Island*, February 17, 1897.

"The 11 August 1966 Friendly Fire on the Point Welcome Forced the Coast Guard, Air Force, and Navy to Work Together in Vietnam." *Naval History* (May/June 1998).

Faust, Harold, and Helen Faust. Personal communication with authors and loan of photographs. 2017–19.

Geer, Terry. Personal communication and loan of photographs of Larry Geer. 2017.

Gibbs, Jim. "Lights of Juan de Fuca Strait and Puget Sound." *West Coast Lighthouses: A Pictorial History of the Guiding Lights of the Sea*. Superior, NE: Superior Publishing, 1974.

———. *Sentinels of the North Pacific*. Hillsboro, OR: Binford and Mort, 1955.

———. *West Coast Lighthouses: A Pictorial History of the Guiding Lights of the Sea*. Superior, NE: Superior Publishing, 1974.

Gilford, Shirley. *Oral History & Archives*. Orcas Island Historical Museum. Eastsound, Washington.

Glidden, Helene. *The Light on the Island*. New York: Coward-McCann. 1951.

———. *The Light on the Island: Collector's Edition: Celebrating the 125th Anniversary of the Patos Island Lighthouse*. Ridgway, CO: San Juan Publishing, 2018.

Goekler, John. "Sentinels of the Sea." *Islands' Weekly*, May 23–30, 1995.

Hagan, Rupert V. Personal communication with Edrie Vinson. 2017–18.

Harrison, Timothy, and Debra Baldwin. "Life and Death at the Doomed." *Lighthouse Digest*. March–April 2016.

Hayward, Orlo E. *Journal of the Light-station at Patos Island*, April 27, 1931– October 8, 1933.

"Helene Glidden Addresses Library Association Group." *Orcas Islander*, December 1954.

Hoffman, Fergus. "'Some Have to Go:' Viet Calls 27." *Seattle Post-Intelligencer*, May 6, 1965.

Jensen, Hans F. *Journal of the Light-station at Patos Island*, December 8, 1922–March 21, 1928.

Johnson, Mandi. "Lighthouse Celebrates 124 Years." *Islands' Sounder*, September 13, 2017.

Journal of the Light-station at Patos Island. 4 volumes, 1893–1933. National Archives and Records Administration.

Journal of the Light-station at Turn Point Stuart Island. February 1897.

La Vergne, Bill. "Patos Bill." *Islands' Sounder*, November 1, 2017.

———. Personal communication. 2017–19.

"Lighthouse Keeper at Blaine Called Suddenly." Bellingham Public Library. N.d. [1919].

Lorenz, Eileen. "Don Fox, 1947-48." *Islands' Sounder*, October 18, 2017. [Correction: 1948–50]

Lougheed, O.J. Personal communication with Edrie Vinson, 2017–19.

Mahler, Harry D. *Journal of Light-station at Patos Island*, December 5, 1893–July 27, 1903.

Morgan, Albert. *Journal of the Light-station at Patos Island*, July 27, 1903–December 7, 1905.

National Archives and Records Administration. Washington, D.C., and Seattle, Washington.

Newport Miner. "Important Happenings of Week from Towns in Our State." January 4, 1912.

Newport News Times. "Sisters Recall Lighthouse Life on Coast." July 7, 1976.

Orcas Island Historical Museum. Various records, photographs. Eastsound, Washington.

Page, Don. "C.G. Tries Out Newest Patrol Boat." *Seattle Times*, July 14, 1962.

Peterson, Douglas. *United States Lighthouse Service Tenders, 1840–1939*. Annapolis, MD. Eastwind Publishing, 2000.

Puget Sound Weekly Argus. "The Wreck of the John Rosenfeld." February 25, 1886.

Register of Visitors: Patos Island Light Station. Orcas Island Historical Museum. Eastsound, Washington. 1903–76.

San Juan Islander. "Farcical Test of Sunday Law." March 14, 1908.

———. "H.D. Mahler Gets Write Up." March 28, 1913.

———. "Heroic Act of Light Keeper." December 29, 1911.

———. "John W. Penson Obituary." January 27, 1911.

———. "Launch Thieves Captured and Sentenced." May 22, 1914.

———. "Patos Island Omitted." July 1908.

———. "Patos to Have Mail Service." August 29, 1908.

———. "The University Marine Station." June 24, 1905.

Seattle Post-Intelligencer. "Many New Lighthouses." May 6, 1890.

———. "Office of U.S. Lighthouse Engineer." August 2, 1892.

———. "Senate Appropriations Bill." June 26, 1890.

———. "Two More Appointments." July 30, 1893.

Seattle Times. "New Patrol Boats: 82-Footers Due This Week." May 20, 1962.

———. "Ships Due for Viet-Nam Duty." May 27, 1965.

Sharman, Chuck. "Naming the Islands Was Everybody's Game." *Journal Springtide* (1979).

Titterington, Clarence. Personal communication with Carla Chalker. May 15, 2009.

U.S. Census. Various dates and various places. Washington, D.C.

U.S. Coast Guard Museum Northwest. Seattle, Washington. Various photographs and documents.

Viking. Orcas Island High School Yearbook. 1946.

Villeneuve, Matthew. "Helene Glidden and Her Lighthouse: A Historical Reading of *The Light on the Island*." Ridgway, CO: San Juan Publishing, 2018.

———. "The Patos Island Lighthouse: A Social History of a Maritime Borderland, 1893–1951." *Pacific Northwest Quarterly* 108, no. 4 (Fall 2017).

Vinson, Edrie. "Celebrating 125 Years of the Patos Island Lighthouse." *Islands' Sounder*, January 3, 2018.

———. "Clarence 'Tee' Titterington, 1951–1953." *Islands' Sounder*, December 2, 2017.

———. "Dale Arlen Nelson, 1954–1956 & 1958–1960." *Islands' Sounder*, November 15, 2017.

———. "A Fourth Order Fresnel Lens for Patos Fog Signal Station." *Islands' Sounder*, August 16, 2017.

———. "Harold Faust, 1960–1962." *Islands' Sounder*, December 20, 2017.

———. "Visitors to Patos Island Lighthouse." *Islands' Sounder*, May 17, 2017.

Vinson, Edrie, and Terri Vinson. "Albert A. Morgan, 2nd Keeper of the Patos Light." *Islands' Sounder*, April 5, 2017.

———. "The Death of Noah Clark, Assistant Keeper of the Patos Light." *Islands' Sounder*, July 19, 2017.

———. "Edward Durgan, 3rd Keeper of the Patos Light." *Islands' Sounder*, May 3, 2017.

———. "George Louis Lonholt, Fourth Keeper of the Patos Light." *Islands' Sounder*, September 20, 2017.

———. "Harry D. Mahler, Keeper of the Patos Light." *Island's Sounder*, March 15, 2017.

———. "Helene Glidden, Author of *The Light on the Island*." *Islands' Sounder*, June 21, 2017.

———. "Louise Mahler, The First Light Keeper's Wife on Patos Island." *Islands' Sounder*, August 2, 2017.

———. "The Patos Island Lighthouse." *Islands' Sounder*, July 5, 2017.

———. "Remembrance." *Islands' Sounder*, November 9, 2016.

———. "San Juan Island Lighthouses." *Islands' Sounder*, February 15, 2017.

———. "The War Years and Patos Island Lighthouse." *Islands' Sounder*, September 6, 2017.

Vinson, Edrie, and Victoria Atkins. "Rupert V. Hagen, Coast Guard WWII, 1943–1945." *Islands' Sounder*, October 4, 2017.

Washington Standard. "Wreck of John Rosenfeld." May 13, 1887.

Washington State Archives. Department of Health. Death Index. Albert Arthur Morgan. November 6, 1918.

———. San Juan County Auditor. Marriage Records. Harry D. Mahler and Louise Rilling. June 26, 1895.

Washington State Board of Health. Bureau of Vital Statistics. Certificate of Death. John Penson. January 15, 1911.

Waters, Criss C. *Journal of the Light-station at Patos Island*, March 23, 1928–April 26, 1931.

White, Margaret. "My First Christmas." Patos Island. Orcas Island Historical Museum. Archives. 1984.

"With McDonald at Patos Island Light Station 1959." *Saltwater People Historical Society*. February 1, 2018.

Websites

Islands Oil Spill Association. iosaonline.org.

Lighthouse Friends. lighthousefriends.com.

Newcastle Island Marine Provincial Park. http://www.env.gov.bc.ca/bcparks/explore/parkpgs/newcastle.

Saltwater People Historical Society. https://saltwaterpeoplehistoricalsociety.blogspot.com.

Washington Rural Heritage. Patos Page. 482 individual entries. 2017–18. washingtonruralheritage.org.

INDEX

ABOUT THE AUTHORS

Edrie Lee Vinson holds a BA degree in history and English from Carroll College in Helena, Montana, and an MA in history and archaeology from Montana State University in Bozeman, Montana. She has worked in historic preservation and in the environmental sciences. Her last assignment was as an environmental project manager for a federal agency. Since retirement, Vinson has volunteered at the Orcas Island Historical Museum in the positions of first vice-president of the board of directors and as museum archivist. Her specialty has been the field of photography, cataloguing the collection into the Past Perfect Museum Database, and scanning photographs for the Washington Rural Heritage website, Orcas Island and Patos Island pages. Currently, she serves as president of the Keepers of the Patos Light, an all-volunteer organization.

Terri Vinson holds a degree in Asian studies, with a focus in history, from the Evergreen State College in Olympia, Washington. She did graduate studies at the University of Hawaii at Manoa, Honolulu, Hawaii. Her interest in local history was inspired by her grandmother Edrie. She began volunteering at the Orcas Island Historical Museum alongside Edrie, doing archival organization and research, and she eventually became the program director for the oral history program. She oversaw the management of a collection of more than one hundred local historic interviews, digitizing and transcribing them for use in an electronic listening kiosk. Terri now serves as the secretary for the Keepers of the Patos Light.